THE ART OF
SUCCESS

Strategies on How to Obtain Your Dreams

DR. DIANE DAVIS PH.D.

Endorsements

After reading "The Art of Success: Strategies on How to Obtain Your Dreams," I now understand if you change your mind and thoughts you change your life. Dr. Davis takes us through the steps of understanding "success thinking" and what success means and what it takes to change your life. We all want to see the world differently, but we can't change the world until we first change ourselves. Dr. Davis says, "life is to know that we each have a unique role to fulfill for ourselves and to serve others while on this earth." Enjoyable read!

> **—Pamela Harris, New York State Assembly**

I recommend this book because it speaks to truth. In our culture, "celebrity and busyness" have become diseases that are killing us. Dr. Davis' excellent book is the best therapy I know of. It is full of wisdom and grace without compromise.

> **—Dr. Princetta Gloria Berry, Retired Psychiatrist, Mt. Sinai Cornell University Medical Center**

The Art of Success: Strategies on How to Obtain Your Dreams plunges into the realm of the unconscious mind and it brings to light the consciousness to fulfill your dreams. It is easy to read. Love the strategies given to achieve your personal success and how to celebrate them as you achieve. It's a must-read.

**—Ruth Morales, Diploma in Christian Education,
Director of Brooklyn Community Services**

After reading, The Art of Success, the charts and guides were most helpful. If readers use these charts and strategies in their personal experiences they will obtain their DREAMS.

**—Robin Sheares,
Acting Justice of New York State Supreme Court**

Dr. Diane Davis books reminds us that success is in our reach. Stay focused, follow these steps and the sky is the limit!

—Bishop Waylyn Hobbs, Jr.

The Art of Success:
Strategies on How to Obtain Your Dreams

ISBN-9798712416831

Printed in the United States of America ©2021 by Dr. Diane Davis, Ph.D.
Second Printing
All Rights Reserved.

You may reach the author at:
ddavis_ddavis99@yahoo.com
or
Dr. Diane Davis
P.O. Box 240 045
Brooklyn, New York 11224

No part of this book may be reproduced or transmitted in any form or by any means, electronic or mechanical, including photocopying, recording, or by any information storage and retrieval system, without permission in writing from the publisher.

DEDICATION

I dedicate this book to my four children Robert, Kimberly, Ryan and Ryshawn. My children have inspired me to write this book and make a better life for myself so that I can take good care of them mentally, physically and spiritually.

ACKNOWLEDGEMENTS

I would like to first and foremost thank god for His wisdom, understanding, and guidance in writing this book.

I know how blessed I am that God brought an extraordinary publisher and agent, Dr. Aaron Lewis into my life to help birth this book. Thank you, Dr. Lewis, for believing in this project. I thank you for your editorial expertise in improving the manuscript and for making this book a reality. I could not have done it alone.

I thank God for my husband Lindsey Davis who supports my vision and dreams. He is my best friend and partner in marriage and business. Lindsey is my soul mate.

I would like to give all praises to God for my beloved parents Dozier and Evelyn Gardner, my grandparents Dozier Sr. and Sallie Gardner and Aunt Willie. Although, they are not physically here, their spirit still lives in me. I thank them for their love and guidance. I take pride in my heritage and in the lingering mental image that has inspired me as a child to write this book.

A special thanks to Dr. Daniel Eckstein, my Ph.D. mentor, who encouraged me to publish my first book.

Thank you Judi Orlando, former Executive Director of Astella Development, and my surrogate mom, and Eric Levy for critiquing the first draft of the manuscript and for encouraging me to publish.

I also owe special thanks to my four children Robert, Kimberly, Ryan and Ryshawn and my five grandchildren Anastasia, Brad, Natalya, Evan and Tatum for keeping my spirit open with love.

I thank my whole wonderful support team of friends who gave me constant support and encouragement to write this book: Elisa Lloyd, Dr. Princette Berry, my spiritual sister, Lisa Lugo, Ron Peterson, Madeline Torres, Arlean Adekoya Dr. Omi, and Nadia Aboawad.

TABLE OF CONTENTS

Introduction..11

Chapter One: Understanding Success....................17

Chapter Two: Purpose......................................29

Chapter Three: Emotional Development and
    Emotional Intelligence............................39

Chapter Four: Soul Searching.................................47

Chapter Five: Who are You?..............................61

Chapter Six: Tradition......................................73

Chapter Seven: Faith..81

Chapter Eight: Reading is Still Fundamental.........87

Chapter Nine: Vision..91

Chapter Ten: Mind..99

Chapter Eleven: Exercise..................................109

Chapter Twelve: Afterword..............................113

INTRODUCTION

"Success is not final; failure is not fatal: It is the courage to continue that counts."
— *Winston S. Churchill*

We all want success. Although some may not admit it, success is the general goal of humanity. Few however, understand the strategies or skills that it takes to master the art of success. To master any skill, whether drawing, singing, litigating, performing surgery or becoming a great orator, one must commit to following a blue print. You hold in your hands the blueprint, the practical guide that will provide you with what you need to know on how to master the necessary art and skills to secure your success in life.

> Success is the general goal of humanity

Webster's Dictionary defines art as a "human effort to imitate, a conscious arrangement or a system of principles and methods used in the performance of a set of activities." Since art is basically a conscious effort to duplicate a system of principles and methods in the performance of a set of activities already in existence, you will find this book exciting to learn the artful strategies. These artful strategies will provide a carefully devised plan of action that can help you achieve your goal. Success people have this in common, they make conscious decisions, based on their desires to achieve something with intent.

Successful people make up their mind to accomplish what they desire. Most successful people do not leave their actions and decisions to chance. They intend to be and become whatever it is that they are believing for. They fervently striving in their desires and dreams and they exercise the faith necessary to achieve them. Successful people also generally tend to be dreamers. And based on their desires and dreams, they forecast with great imagination the vision for whatever they expect to achieve in life.

They connect their imagination with persistence as they devise a plan to set in motion, while allowing the universe to work in divine order that which will bring their images or imagination into physical reality. For many years now, I have studied and observed others. I've seen how some have sincerely strived for success, yet they've seemingly failed. After that failure, it became harder and harder. Then I discovered that the reason it became harder is because either myself or others failed to recognize that there are clues to success. I failed to realize then that success is not something that happens overnight, but rather it is something that is cultivated over time.

Think about a farmer, who cultivates the soil and prepares it for seeding. After that, he or she will plant seed into the soil. Then the farmer will feed the soil with fertilizer and other soil-rich nutrients. When the soil is parched from the sun, the farmer will water the soil at night until . . . the plant peeks through the soil and begins to stand tall. There are processes to

> Success is not something that happens over night, but it is rather something that is cultivated over time

"becoming" in life. Frustration comes when one either tries to avoid or rush the process. With success it is the same. There are daily tasks that you must commit to in order to gain success in life.

Success is not like playing the lottery, but it is, rather, a system, a daily commitment to reinventing your life. In your hands are a series of daily success tasks that I have mastered over the years. And now I am freely sharing them with you. I've practiced these tasks and have also shared many of these daily habits with my clients over the years as a mental health counselor. Not only did they work for me but they also proved to be remarkably effective with my clients as well, which proves that success can be transferable if one is willing to do the work.

As you continue to read and begin to practice the truths in this book you will begin to experience the wealth, respect, sense of contribution, or whatever desired result you are seeking. Far too often, people tend to define success through narrow lenses: having more money, wearing the latest designer clothing, owning an exotic car, or living in a mansion. While those things are not inherently negative, those things alone are not success at all. Success is not materialistic. Success often produces material trappings, but the trappings are not success. True success is the ability to look within oneself and make the necessary changes to become self-sufficient.

Success always begins within. When you have achieved internal self-sufficient skills that is when all your external desires will become a reality. Success will always mean different things to different people. Success may have different meanings for people living in different regions. For a Wall Street broker, success may be defined as having a highly profitable day on the market. For a homeless person, success may be defined as finding a place to stay the night. This book is not about convincing you to see success the way that I do. However you define success is fine.

My job is to help you to reach your success goals, whatever they may be. My request is that you stay open-minded throughout this process. Follow the daily suggestions in this book and incorporate them into your lifestyle. On this journey you will become acquainted with the real you. You will begin to recognize more easily what is

> True success is the ability to look within oneself and make the necessary changes to become self-sufficient

right from what is wrong in your world and develop the courage to confront it head on. Like driving a car or even learning how to ride a bicycle, success is a learned behavior that when practiced correctly will become second nature to you. My goal for you is to become a master of success so that success will come to you without you even thinking about it— second-nature success.

CHAPTER ONE

Understanding Success

"There are no secrets to success. It is the result of preparation, hard work, and learning from failure."
—*Colin Powell*

Take a few minutes to think about what success means to you. Don't feel pressured or locked into a certain definition. Success means very different things depending on the person and their situation. For LeBron James or Stephen Curry success may mean winning the NBA Championship and bringing home a ring. For Mother Teresa success meant living her entire life, selflessly giving back to the children and families in Calcutta, India. Those are obviously two very different

> Success should not be looked at as an end, but rather a steady process of evolving from one state to another

examples of success. But what does success mean to you? Get an image of success and hold that thought in your mind.

After you have thought about what success means to you compare it to the two following definitions. The Merriam-Webster Dictionary defines success as the fact of getting or achieving wealth, respect, or fame; the correct or desired result of an attempt. Webster's New World Dictionary defines success as a favorable or satisfactory outcome or result. Based on these descriptions, success is having achieved anything hoped for that provided you a favorable outcome. Alternative medicine advocate and author of The Seven Spiritual Laws of Success, Deepak Chopra, describes success as a journey rather than a destination. From that point of view success should not be looked at as an end, but rather a steady process of evolving from one state to another.

Success—A Journey to Somewhere

Success is a journey that takes determination to set a plan in your consciousness. Once the plan is set, action steps must be taken to produce an effect to reach your objectives and goals. When a person sets goals and objectives, those goals and objectives become the compass to get whatever is desired. Objectives are things that you do to reach your goals. For example: the objective to earning a degree is to pass all the required classes. The student objectives are to maintain B grades in math, science, history and all major courses to obtain his or her Bachelor of Science degree. We need to complete the necessary objectives to achieve our goal.

A goal is the result of your efforts. It is an aim that you want to achieve. Successful people understand the importance of working toward achieving an objective. One of the major differences between those that are successful and those that are not is that successful people thrive and push harder in difficult times. Unsuccessful people often give up at the first sign of opposition or challenge. For the successful, challenges and tests becomes a rite of passage for them. The greater the challenge the greater the victory is the creed of those that succeed.

Successful people tend to be optimistic people. Whether they consciously recognize it or not, they live by a faith code. They believe in the substance of things unseen but hoped for. *Now faith is the substance of things hoped for, the evidence of things not seen. Hebrews 11:1* (KJV). For this reason, they continue to reach their goals in life. They continue to set goals and objectives. These goals and objectives becomes the driving force or, shall I say, the *life* force behind everything they do. So, if you want new life, new life comes in the form of making new plans for yourself. New life comes in the form of setting new objectives and goals for yourself.

> Successful people thrive and push harder in difficult times

Have you ever seen someone start a new career after finishing a different one? Or have you seen someone quit their previous position in their forties to start an entirely new profession? If you have, this is an example of a person creating new life for him or herself. This is the habit of the successful, to always create new paths by creating new goals, achieving them, and then creating new ones. Today can be the beginning of a new life for you. But it begins with writing down your goals and objectives.

On a separate piece of paper, I want you to write down in it might be better to write the word four rather than the number 4. Beside each goal column, I want you to put an objective column with projected time frames next to it. In the remaining column, I want you to write a date down for when you believe you will accomplish each one. You may be thinking that you are not sure about the accomplishment date. Don't worry about accuracy at this point. The reason you need to put a target date down is to give yourself the push needed to move closer toward your goals. Without dating your goals, you may never reach them. Look at the graph below and try to follow the pattern. This is your life, so remember to write what you like and what you desire.

Here's an example of what your goals may look like:

Short Term Goal	Objectives	Date That I'll Achieve It	Long Term Goal	Objectives	Date That I'll Achieve It
Purchase 2 rental properties	Look at several properties each week to purchase	December 2017	Net worth portfolio of $1,000,000	To create multiple streams of income	January 2022
To lose 12 pounds	Daily exercise, Proper eating plan	October 2017	Pay off student loans	All money over my expenses, savings and investments will go toward loans	November 2023

I Feel Good

In 1964, singer and dancer James Brown released a single entitled I Got You (I Feel Good). This song soared to the top of the music charts and became his bestselling and most popular song ever. The actual title is "I Got You." The subtitle is "I Feel Good." What people around the world most remember about that song is "I Feel Good." In fact, most people believe that is the name of the song. The reason this song became so popular is because people wanted a reason to feel good.

In 1964, there was a great amount of civil and racial unrest in America might sound a little better. Violence was widespread and fear was in the air. In July of the same year Lyndon B. Johnson signed The Civil Rights Act of 1964. While segregation was still widely in effect, James Brown wanted to shift the focus from the negative to the positive. He believed that if you feel good then you are good. His goals were set on being an international success. And Mr. Brown went on to accomplish just that, being forever known as the Godfather of Soul and a progenitor of funk music.

Feeling good is a major element to being a success in life. You must feel good about your actions on your journey to success. Esther and Jerry Hicks, authors of <u>The Law of Attraction</u> noted that strong good feelings will bring new evidence into your existence. Having good feelings can attract your desires and dreams, and bring them into your reality. If you truly want to bring a desire or dream into your reality you must feel it as if you already have it. Claim it and it will be yours very soon.

Dr. David Che, author of <u>Total Law of Attraction: Unleash Your Secret Creative Power to Get What You Want</u>, concurred with the Hicks, that when you think of a desire with strong feelings you are putting your awareness on the wave. Che noted that if a person believes or expects the wave, then the wave will become a reality. Each time a desired goal or objective becomes a

> Feeling good is a major element to being a success in life

reality, check it off your list and begin working on the next one. It is also important that when you reach your goals and objectives to reward yourself. Celebrate yourself. A great part of success is celebration.

Go get your hair done. Get a manicure and pedicure. Get a full body massage. Buy a new outfit. Treat yourself to dinner with your favorite person. Plan a vacation overseas. Celebrating your success is a motivating factor to continue your journey toward reaching other goals. Celebrating yourself also sends your brain a healthy message that success is good and well worth the effort set forth in achieving it.

Professor and love expert, Dr. Leo Buscaglia said, "We have to be ready to risk, look inside ourselves and proceed through trial and error. The job will be mainly ours." We are required to be our own mentors. You do not need motivation from others. You can stimulate your own mind with thoughts of enthusiasm and engrossing, strong desires. It may not be easy for you at first, but with daily practice it will eventually become part of you. "Self-control is key to focused practice – which is necessary for the development of any skill – since deliberate practice is about pushing yourself to do the most difficult things," says Michael Bond.

Practice daily visualizing your end result (goal). Practice being happy while you work toward each objective until you reach your goal. When you practice happy feelings as you work, you send positive emotions into the universe and the universe responds to those feelings. As you practice these steps believe that you are allowing the end results to become reality. It takes determination, dedication, motivation and daily practice. "You won't get far without the ability to persevere and stay committed to far-off goals, or grit," says Michael Bond. All you have to do is choose your future goals in your mind.

Once you have chosen your future goals, visualize them, develop self-control, and become self-motivated so that you can make plans without being directed by others, then you should close your eyes to imagine your goal as being reality. Feel happy, as if you have already achieved your goals, be determined to reach your goals despite any difficulties and you will see your goal soon become a reality.

The Power of Vision

Vision is a motivational factor that helps successful people to reach their goals. A vision is energy in your heart. It has power. Your vision has the limitless capabilities to get you more or less of anything that you desire. You can actually see your desire as if it already exists. Your vision has an intensity of power that drives you to the person or thing that you most desire. This source of power will allow you to go beyond your natural capacity to act. Your vision is a mental picture in your brain that creates a powerful vibration.

The built-in natural and spiritual abilities imparted to you give you the transmitting power allowing the universe to bring your vision to reality.

When I was a young girl, I created a scrapbook of my dream home. My father had beautiful interior decorating books and magazines in our home library. I used to cut the pictures out and paste them in my scrapbook. For many years, I would gaze daily at the pictures in my scrapbook and I visualized myself living in that space. I would play jazz on my phonograph in my bedroom while I fingered through my scrapbook.

> Your vision has the limitless capabilities to get you more of or less of anything that you desire

I would have back and forth conversations with my imaginary husband and children. It felt so good living out of the picture in my scrapbook. Today I am living my childhood vision. I'm living the real-life version of my vision. Visions really do come true. Sometimes, when I am cleaning my home I experience déjà vu. Literally, I have strong sensations as I'm cleaning my home as though it happened in a past reality.

Since I had lived this out in my mind as a child, I am living it over again. Dr. Che identified this experience as the subconscious mind that sends your desires up to the Ether, or as some may say to God or aHigher Power. In physics, the scientific study of physical forces and qualities notes that the ether is electromagnetic waves of current carrying coil which magnetizes. Dr. Che further revealed that once the subconscious mind enters the Ether (God/Higher

Power/electromagnetic waves) it attracts similar vibrational energies.

The similar vibrational energies return to the physical world and show up in your circumstances. Astounding! So, as it relates to your success in life, it is important for you to visualize your desire with a strong emotion attached to it so that your innate abilities may grant you your desire. Your built-in natural and spiritual power has unlimited resources to bring all your desires or dreams to fruition. All you need is a vision, good feelings, and a strong desire to bring the results into your reality.

> Your built-in natural and spiritual power has unlimited resources to bring all your desires or dreams to fruition

True Success is All About Risk-Taking

It is important for successful people to visualize how they desire their lives to fully play out. As important as visualization is, so is the willingness to take risks in life. There is no such thing as real success without risks. Often, people shy away from taking risks because of the fear of failure. Truthfully,, you will never become successful without risks and failures. Success is built upon the blocks of risk-taking and many failures. No one really learns much from their successes in life. As I mentioned earlier, success is a celebratory experience. However, you will learn from your experience. If you don't learn the first go 'round, you'll learn the second time.

Failure is a lesson. Failure is inadequate growth or inadequate production of something. When you experience failure, it is usually because you are viewing something unclearly. No matter how hard failure may strike you, you must look for what you need to improve. Failure signifies a breakdown of something. It says that there is something missing. Ask yourself, what is missing or what appears to be irretrievably broken down in your life? Meditate on ways to reverse the breakdown. Try to meditate on solutions for about 20 minutes daily. Carefully listen to the internal voice to give you answers.

God or your Higher Power will speak to you and give you the answers that you are searching for. Failures are the spirit's way of compelling you to make changes. Sometimes you are forced to do away with old habits. You may need to learn a new way of doing something. By learning from your failures, you will gain greater strength and confidence to do something you desire, even greater than before. In time, failure will no longer feel like inadequate growth. You will realize that the failures were needed to learn lessons, to make necessary adjustments so you can live your life to the fullest.

My help cometh from the Lord, which made heaven and earth. Psalms121:2

Failure is a lesson

CHAPTER TWO

Purpose

The purpose of human life is to serve, and to show compassion and the will to help others.
—*Albert Schweitzer*

The purpose of life is to know that we each have a unique role to fulfill for ourselves and to serve others while on this earth. Each of us has been given natural ability and supernatural gifts. Our natural gifts are given to us at birth and cultivated throughout life. Our spiritual gifts are imparted to us during our spiritual rebirth. To truly understand your purpose, you must seek your God and His/Her divine helper to be your guide. You must be spiritually centered. What I mean by spiritually centered is that you must look deep inside yourself and become connected to the spirit. A greater part of your purpose is to realize that you are one with the spirit and have always been connected.

When you become aligned with the spirit you become increasingly occupied with divine things, as opposed to worldly things. This process is the genesis of true and lasting success. The spirit cannot be seen with human eyes or touched with human hands. It can only be felt internally. As you meditate in spirit, you may experience a tingling within. The

> A greater part of your purpose is to realize that you are one with Spirit and have always been connected

Spirit manifests itself in different ways. The spirit is divine. It is positive energy and is aspiring to influence your soul. The spirit of God, who is your divine helper, is always there for you.

As written in the Holy Qur'an (The Most High) "we must glorify the name of the Lord, the most high, who creates, then makes complete, and who makes (things) according to a measure, then guides (them to their goal)." Ultimately, it is God who offers guidance and direction. The spirit of God leads you towards the fulfillment of your goals in life. Keep your mind toward God. God's manifest presence will give you His glory to be strengthened and reinforced with mighty power in your inner self. We are God's people. Therefore, live your life with the full armor of your divine power.

Right Alignment

He who walks with wise men will be wise, But the companion of fools will be destroyed. Proverbs 13:20

You are the company that you keep. In time, you become likened to your surroundings. Shield yourself from debilitating influences by staying clear of people who do not share your spirituality or those who oppose God's plan for your life. Safeguarding yourself from people that do not share your spirituality will keep you spiritually sound. This is extremely important because it will keep you in close contact with God. It will also help to keep you focused on your goals and vision.

Tapping into and staying connected with your source ensures that you will always succeed. Your success is determined by how closely connected you are to spirit. You cannot afford to abort that process by allowing the wrong people into your space. Who is the wrong person for you? Anyone who opposes, fights, or tries to tear down your purpose is the wrong person for you. Anyone who does not fully support your purpose is not right for you. Those who fail to see the promise of your purpose in your life and those who do not contribute to your purpose can both be added into the "do not fit" category.

Do not force relationships. Your success in life is purpose driven and follows a natural flow. It is never forced. Spirit simply allows it to happen. That is when

> You are the company that you keep

you are in the right alignment. We each have been put here on earth for a purpose. The purpose in life is to make meaning of your life experiences so far, and to engage in thought processes and activities that coincide with greater well-being, and that will help you to recover from negative experiences and to move forward.

> Do not force relationships

My Grandmother—A Woman of Purpose

When my grandmother Sallie Slaughter-Gardner was alive she'd say to me, "Perhaps my purpose in life is to care for my family and to make sure none of them are homeless." I thought her words were profound because she fully understood her purpose. Because of that she lived a successful life on her terms. Her life was full of happiness. She would tell me stories about her childhood, the traumatic experiences of racism contrasted by beautiful family experiences. She was able to give meaning to her life experiences.

She used her church as an anchor, participating in activities that helped her to recover from negative childhood experiences. That helped to move her forward. She was great in many capacities; as a wife, mother, grandmother, aunt, cousin, friend and usher at her church. My grandmother prayed often, seeking her inner power to guide her. In her, I saw strength, courage, love for humanity and spirituality. She was a loving, caring empathetic and spiritual woman whose sole purpose was to love and care for her family.

Grandma made sure each family member had food to eat and a warm home to live in regardless of their age.

Although I didn't live with my grandmother, every time I saw her she was always in a divine state. Every time I went to visit grandma, I knew that I was going to be loaded up with words of wisdom and spiritual advice. I clearly remember one day when I was sitting at my grandmother's kitchen table having a cup of coffee with her. She was talking about God's guidance. While she was talking, I could literally feel a divine transfer of spirit come upon me. In that moment, I know that God entered my life in a most unusual way.

As I reflect on my childhood, it was my grandmother who taught me about God and the moving of the spirit. Everything that I have experienced in my life has been from my habitual focus on the spirituality that was passed down from my grandmother. Her example showed me the power of purpose in life and how purpose is directly connected to your success in life. Some people relegate purpose to only high-profile positions in life such as being a CEO of a Fortune 500 corporation, or being the President of the United States, or even being a superstar singer like Beyonce.

While all those professions are remarkable, my grandmother's choice to be the best grandmother, nurturer, provider, and spiritual example stands above them all. She may not have made millions or led thousands of people. However, she stayed

> Purpose is directly connected to your success in life

in her lane and and completely fulfilled her purpose. When you completely fulfill your purpose in life, you are a super success! Had I not had my grandmother in my life, I may not have understood just how powerful purpose is.

It's Never Too Late

Perhaps you may be thinking that you are too old to embrace this level of spiritual teaching. I received it as a child from my grandmother. The truth is that there is no time frame to learn how to be spiritual. Whether you are ten years young or one hundred years young it really does not matter. What's most important is that you open your spirit to whatever possibility God has for you. Admit that there is a divine spirit greater than you, and that you are seeking divine help. Call upon your Higher Power to intervene and your spirit will open.

New revelations will come to you. New knowledge, understanding and wisdom will now flow in your life. Some people are bound by negative pasts and negative habits that lead to toxic lifestyles. In an instant, you can really change your inner self and get rid of the toxins within. Go within yourself and believe that God's power is a gift to you. Pray, ask, seek, and watch the miracles of life open up to you.

> Personal effectiveness is also the foundation for people with a purpose

A person with a purpose understands them self. They also know where they are supposed to be in life. The person of purpose has a character of strength, a distinctive and a positive personality. She views herself as a person of great faith in her God/Higher Power, is determined to reach specific goals, has self-respect, self-confidence, compassion, is highly motivated, creative, and has courage and will power.

Personal effectiveness is also the foundation for people with a purpose. They want to share their discoveries and knowledge with the world. Being concerned for others is an important factor for people with a purpose. Truly successful people cannot withhold goodness. They are compelled to share and to give to others everywhere they go. These individuals are committed to promoting goodness in themselves, their family, community and world. Regardless of age, they know for sure it's never too late to live optimal lives, living with purpose and passion.

It is this knowledge of one's ability to contribute to a universal, continual and infinite productivity that adds special meaning to our lives and the courage of our mortality
—Dr. Buscaglia, 1982

Purpose Leads to Better Health

There is growing evidence from research studies that suggest that people who have a greater sense of purpose in life are linked to better health outcomes (Schaefer, Boylan, Reekum, Lapate, Norris, Ryff and Davidson, 2013). A study on adults ages 36 to 84 years, from a MIDUS study (Midlife in the United States), examined whether purpose in life was associated with better emotional recovery following negative picture stimuli.

The study's findings showed that after two years the adults had improved recovery from negative stimuli, indexed by a smaller eye blink after negative pictures offset and other well-being dimensions. The conclusion gained from the study was that adults with a purpose in life were protected from negative emotions and presented resilience through enhanced automatic emotional regulation. The evidence in this study showed that purpose in life is important for improved health and developmental achievement.

Knowing your purpose and living in purpose leads to good health. Love also promotes healthy living. My father taught me to love myself at a young age. Self-love is to love and to know one-self. You will never be able to adequately and healthily love anyone until you first love yourself. Confess out loud, "I love me first." Say it again. Make that your daily mantra and say it at least twice each day. Feel it in your heart. Place good emotions to those words, "I love me first." Believe that the higher power will bring you self-love. As you communicate self-love to yourself, it will communicate between the part of your mind where your conscious thoughts take place and will serve as the seat of action for your subconscious mind.

When you practice love, and become understanding, your self-doubt disappears. When that happens, your self-esteem is strengthened, your character is developed, and your determination to reach dreams becomes a reality. You have the internal strength to make the transition from self-doubt to self-love if you simply trust in your God, love yourself, and believe you have a purpose in life. You must act on the words of guidance within or through intuition— it will give you the best results to embrace your full potential and to find your purpose. The only reason people wander aimlessly in life is because they do not know what their purpose is. Once they discover it, they will find all the fulfillment and happiness they were seeking.

> Knowing your purpose and living in purpose leads to good health

"Perhaps the purpose of life is to forward it by being something, having it make a difference that our unique selves were present.'"

—Leo T. Buscaglia, PhD

CHAPTER THREE

Emotional Development and Emotional Intelligence

"Holding on to anger is like grasping a hot coal with the intent of throwing it at someone else: you are the one who gets burned."
—*Buddha*

Success in life has many compartments, as there are many things, when working together that will produce your desired results. Just like a car has many parts: the engine, transmission, the tires, rims, and driveshaft. That's a short list of what makes up a car. But in order to work and to move from one point to the next, the part that I mentioned must be in working order, otherwise that car will not move forward. Such is the case with your emotional development and your emotional intelligence. Since these elements are crucial to experience healthy success, let's take a quick look at what they are and how they may be connected to your success.

Emotional development is your ability to express, recognize, and manage your feelings at various stages of life. It also involves having empathy for others. How these emotions mature depends largely upon how you may have interacted with your parents, siblings, and peers in your developmental stages. These emotions can be positive or negative. What matters most is that you have matured to a point where you are able to successfully manage those emotions to navigate to the place in life you want to be. Emotional intelligence is the capacity to be in control of your emotions and to handle interpersonal relationships with empathy, justice, and wisdom.

Peter M. Senge (1990) is an American scientist and lecturer. Senge noted that full emotional development offers the greatest degree of leverage in attaining our full potential. Researchers have found that emotional development has been an increasing concern for the last two decades from the general public and the scientific community (Brasseur, Gregoire, Bourdu and Mikolajczak, 2013). Emotional development is better known as "Emotional Intelligence."This concept refers to how people identify and perceive their emotions accurately, express emotions, understand and regulate their own emotions and the emotions of others (Brasseur al et., 2013), and how people promote their own emotional and intellectual growth (Camilleri, Caruana, Falzon and Muscat, 2012).

Intelligence Doesn't Happen Overnight

Muscles take time to build. Careers take years to cultivate. People with physical or mental challenges may take decades to experience meaningful progress. While these endeavors may possibly take less time, in most cases it is expected that it will take a reasonable amount of time to see results. The same is true of emotional intelligence. Emotional intelligence is a process. It doesn't develop overnight. So, one must be patient to receive the maximum results. There are three motivational factors necessary to acquire emotional intelligence: psychological health, physical health and social relationships. At the psychological level, you must have high self-esteem, a sense of well-being, be satisfied with life, and have a decreased risk of developing psychological symptoms (Brasseur al et., 2013). You also must be aware of and understand your own and other's emotions.

On the physical level, you must have less symptoms of stress and psychological disorders. Brasseaur al et., (2013) further noted that you should "not adopt health damaging behaviors, such as smoking and excessive drinking." These may inhibit your success, especially if these behaviors are controlling your emotional states. The idea is that you must be in control of yourself. Finally comes the social level. You must surround yourself with positive people. Negative people and negativity in general have a draining and debilitating effect not only on the body, but on human progress. So, the people with whom you choose to interact daily must be carefully accessed and selected.

> Emotional intelligence is a process

Take a Look at Yourself

When you have mastered the three motivational factors to obtain emotional stability, it will lead to more meaningful and intimate relationships. People who seek emotional intelligence are constantly searching within themselves to understand their feelings and behaviors. This is necessary in that progress within you requires self-evaluation. An often-practiced improper way of assessment is outward. Many people are inclined to look at the behavior of others, to judge others, and to criticize others' lack of progress. This only serves as a smokescreen to hide the one who should be criticized: yourself.

Self-evaluation is an often-painful process. Most people do not enjoy looking at themselves in the mirror, being honest about shortcomings and areas in need of improvement in their lives. However, you cannot skip this step as it is a crucial step towards emotional stability. When human beings allow their subconscious mind to recall negative and positive childhood experiences, it allows them to understand their current emotions and behaviors. It helps them to know and more clearly understand who they are and who they've become. No matter how hard you try to forget your experiences, you cannot take them away.

> People who seek emotional intelligence are constantly searching within themselves to understand their feelings and behaviors

What happened is real. However, you can rename your experiences in life so that they will not have a destructive effect on you. Learn to accept your life's experiences, whether good or bad. By doing so you are confronting life head on and accepting your emotions. This helps to develop emotional intelligence and emotional strength. Accepting the experience(s) is the first step to recovery from emotional damage and emotional depletion. At times experiences can be devastating, so much so that people often believe they can never live through them. The truth is that there is always someone else experiencing a similar or worst situation. And you are just as strong and just as worthy as they are. If they can navigate through it, so can you.

> Most people do not enjoy looking at themselves in the mirror

Get the Help You Need

Remember that you are never alone. You are destined for success. Remember that success is not an individual sport, it's a team effort. Join a support group in your community. Support groups have people with similar issues who help emotionally and socially strengthen one another. They share personal experiences, coping strategies, and resources, and provide sympathy and understanding. Support groups help you to identify with another person's experiences. Through that identification, you can help yourself and others through the process.

I believe trials and tribulations are God's way of testing our strength. They do not come to destroy us, just test us. This is God's way of teaching valuable lessons. Take time to listen to the voice within. You will begin to learn and understand your internal environment. In understanding your internal environment, you will be able to plan for and manage change. Change is good. It allows you to access all your experiences, the good, bad, right, wrong, and the devastating ones, accept themand continue to move forward. You are responsible for change in your life. Accept it and own it. Begin to say, "Only I am responsible for change in my life." After that, say, "I have the power to produce powerful and lasting change in my life, because I am in control of my emotions."

> "Only I am responsible for change in my life."

When you really want change in your life and you really desire to get the help you need to move forward, you must be honest with yourself. You must admit first that you have disturbed emotions. To change the disturbed emotions, you need to reflect on how and what led to them in the first place. This will teach you where the source of your anger, anxiety and other disturbed emotions came from. Once you understand your disturbed emotions, you must modify your cognitions. This is done through meditation techniques, which may also help to decrease anxiety.

Walking, jogging and other kinds of physical activities are also very helpful. When you are relaxed your body, mind and emotions begin to practice self-statements. Self-statements are merely new things that you say to yourself. For example: "I am angry that my partner left me for another woman." I must accept it, deal with my abandonment issues and say to myself, "I am doing well, despite the fact my partner has left me. The relationship was not meant for me. I know my divine helper will send the right partner for me." Self-statements give the power and control back to you.

Begin practicing self-statements daily to change any wavering emotions. After you have mastered practicing self-statements, begin to make the necessary changes to improve your situation. Do not forget to help someone less fortunate than you to overcome his or her pains. Remember, success is a team effort. We are all in this together. Helping someone else is part of the process of helping yourself. Each person who is blessed by this process should make a commitment to help another person. Your divine helper will continue to help you as long as you help others. What you put into the universe the universe will always bring it back to you—multiplied.

CHAPTER FOUR

Soul Searching

Put your heart, mind, and soul into even your smallest acts.
This is the secret of success.
—*Swami Sivananda*

Soul searching is key in human development. It involves self-exploration in the quest to discover real meaning in life. Soul searching is an act of inner knowledge of the soul. It provides internal healing and helps in finding your purpose in life. It is a deep and intentional assessment of one's emotions and motives. Succinctly put, soul searching helps you to know whether you are on the correct path or not. In a quiet and still way, the universe connects you to your divine helper, who in turn delivers you to your divine purpose. The all-providing source of all our lives is in control of the universe and everything in it.

When you pray, or meditate to your divine helper, a still small voice will guide you either in words or in hunches that will push you forward. Your divine power will guide you to restructure your spirit in the light of understanding and new experiences. The still small voice will become your teacher, leading you into a life of purpose, love and action that will in time become the guide, helping you to create your desires and dreams.

Making the Connection

Successful people are people who regularly practice soul searching. Dennis P. Kimbro, author of What makes the Great Great noted, "As we respond to the higher impulses of the soul, we become the man or woman we were truly meant to be – true masters of the universe." It is only when we search our innermost soul that we truly find ourselves. We all have a purpose in life. Therefore, a search for the soul is essential before understanding your true self.

There are two important components you must experience before you begin soul searching: (1) you must have a belief in a divine helper, and (2) have a personal relationship with your divine helper. Dr. Jared Kass, professor of counseling and psychology at Lesley University, has conducted research on spiritual maturation. He noted that engagement in these two essential components has been related to an evolving ability for spiritual cognitions and aware-

> Successful people are people who regularly practice soul searching

ness, which has been known to connect with one's divine helper. From this point of view, searching for your soul is a personal learning process of having the cognitive ability to believe and clarify that there is a force more powerful than yourself, and that you have the capacity to begin building a relationship with that divine power.

Soul searching is not an arduous task. It can be accomplished through daily prayer, meditation or reading affirmations from the Bible, the Torah, the Holy Qur'an or any spiritual book that resonates with you. When you begin your process, recognize that this process is very different for each person. To reach a summit experience it may take a day, week, month, or years. There is really no way to measure how long it will be before you reach maturation. The most important thing is patience. You will know and feel within yourself when you have reached where you want to be.

There are no two people created exactly alike. Therefore, you will have a uniquely different experience. Focus only on your own innermost soul. Listen closely to the voice inside; it is your personal guide. This is a powerful process. The inner voice will guide you and your prayers will be answered. Successful people are open and ready to respond to the voice inside. With daily practice, the process will become simpler. Like the R&B group "The Whispers'" hit song suggests, it "Just Gets Better With Time."

Creating Your Private Space

Each day you should set aside some quiet time for soul searching. It is important that you are alone. Find a place where there are no distractions. Put your cell phone on silent. Turn off your television, your computer or anything that may potentially distract you. Relax, close your eyes, practice breathing exercises (inhale slowly through your nostrils and exhale slowly through your mouth). Begin to meditate by keeping the focus on the center of your forehead. Use your imagination. If you can, find a place with natural surroundings such as the ocean, a mountain, or a park with beautiful trees. Allow your thoughts to flow freely. As you do this, you will begin to experience great results.

Listen as your inner voice speaks to you. I find that early in the morning approximately 5 a.m. works best for me to meditate. It's the perfect time to shut out noise before the hectic demands of the day begin. Early mornings are the most tranquil for me. You may be different. Find a time of the day that best works for you. During this time, begin to create a love space between you and your God. See God as your divine helper. Listen intently for instructions that He has for you for your day, your week, your month or year. God is always speaking and giving loving directions. You must be ready to receive all that He has for you.

> God is always speaking and giving loving directions. You must be in a position to receive all that Has for you

The soft voice of God doesn't speak in a brash or loud tone, but always gently to your inner self. I believe He speaks softly to command your full and total attention. He wants your undivided attention and speaks low so that you will be inclined to listen carefully, closely, and personally. This private space is an intimate space with God. Be open to the blessings that are set for you. After learning how to live a spiritual life, I became rich in the spirit.

The spirit helped me to develop rational thinking skills about complex situations that I was experiencing and the cognitive ability to make better decisions. This profound state of spiritual awareness was such an overwhelming, wonderful feeling. It provided me with a feeling of internal richness. That richness was far greater than any physical riches that I have ever acquired. It all began with me putting my private world in order, and creating a space designed solely for intimacy between me and my God.

Hearing and Doing

But don't just listen to God's word. You must do what it says. Otherwise, you are only fooling yourselves. James 1:22 NLT

After experiencing these profound encounters with the spirit, I began daily meditations, listening to the still small voice within myself, experiencing sensations traveling in my body, and reading my Bible. It was then that I began to recognize that all my life improvements and all my success came as a direct result of my soul searching. One morning around 3 a.m., during sleep time, I remember hearing a soft voice whisper, "Diane, get up and go buy a house." I woke up out of my sleep scared and confused. As I looked around the room I was all-alone.

Although I felt a bit confused by the prompting, I remained open to the spirit. My grandmother Sallie taught me that when the Holy Spirit speaks, never ignore His voice as you may miss your blessings. In that moment, I felt an overwhelming sense of gratefulness. I was grateful that God would even consider me to receive His directions.

Being reared in a religious family, I would always hear my grandmother and other family members talk about God and the Holy Spirit. They would always remind me to listen to and obey the spirit. As a result, I understood how to embrace the moment with reverential fear. I wasn't fearful in the sense of being scared, but rather holding the moment with a sense of respect and admiration. If it was truly God speaking then I wanted to be sure to do what he said.

At that time, I was living in a high-rise housing development with so many rodents running around my apartment. It was a horrible experience. My three small children were all suffering with bronchial asthma caused by sub-standard living conditions. The rodents triggered respiratory problems in my children and they were breathing with great difficulty and coughing a lot. My children suffered with medical problems stemming from the apartment. Even worse, I began to develop psychological complications as I began to live in constant fear. It was as I was sitting, fearful, in my living room, that I heard God giving me clear instructions.

The voice within told me that I no longer had to live in fear and that I should go to Astella Development and purchase a home. Knowing my financial state, it didn't make sense to me. But I knew that I wasn't hearing things so I went in faith anyway. At 9:00 a.m., I went to the local community-based organization, Astella Development, to inquire about purchasing a home. Mrs. Judi Orlando, the executive director of the organization, helped to walk me through the application process. Mrs. Orlando introduced me to their mortgage consultant who then assisted me with securing a mortgage. Within six months, I was in a brand new home.

The power of prayer coupled with listening to the voice of God opened doors of new opportunity for me and my children. After several months of living in our new home, I observed that my children's breathing had improved and they no longer had bronchial asthma. My psychological challenges greatly improved. Successful people are responsive to the voice of God. Napoleon

> You may be able to argue and debate about a person's beliefs or creeds, but you cannot dispute a person's personal experience

Hill, author of Think and Grow Rich, noted in his book that human beings do receive truthful knowledge, through resources other than physical senses.

Successful people that I have interviewed who have experienced hearing the still small voice and who were responsive to that voice, indicated that it was their belief in a higher power and their personal relationship with their higher power that made it possible to be responsive to the voice. Successfulpeople know that there is a power greater than humans. They know it to be true, because they have experienced it. You may be able to argue and debate about a person's beliefs or creeds, but you cannot dispute a person's personal experience. In my experience, each time I've heard the voice of God within I listened, obeyed and received. If you begin to do the same, I believe you'll experience the joy of hearing, doing, and receiving just as I have.

Tapping into your Truest Self

Successful people's identities transcend the material realm. They relate to the universe and the spirit world with even more intensity than the physical world. When you begin to understand your full potential in life you will know that you have been given a unique opportunity to connect intimately with the God and the universe. God is spirit. You cannot physically touch God. In the same manner you also are spirit, that is the real you. When you close your eyes, you may feel its presence. The spirit contains light that directs your paths. It is like having a built-in navigational system.

Trust in the LORD with all your heart, and lean not on your own understanding; In all your ways acknowledge Him, And He shall direct your paths. Proverbs 3:5-6

This mediation process will guide you to the still small voice of God. **Step One:** Go into a room and sit quietly without any disturbance. **Step Two:** Close your eyes, and breathe in through your nose and release each breath slowly through your mouth. Do this meditation for 15 minutes until you feel totally relaxed. **Step Three:** As your eyes are closed and your body has reached a level of relaxation; focus your attention on images of mountains, forests, a beautiful park, an ocean or your favorite place. Remain focused on this scenery for 15 minutes.

As you are relaxing, your mind may wander to different thoughts. Say to yourself, "I have no thoughts." Clear your mind of any disturbing thoughts. **Step Four:** Listen quietly for the soft still voice. Great results will prevail. The voice of your divine helper is full of love, care and encouragement. The words will comfort and guide you. "Trusting not on your understanding" is key to opening your soul. The soul is a non-physical aspect of you. Continue to meditate and follow the four steps that were described above so that the God of your understanding will provide the substance that you are striving to believe in.

Spiritual people train themselves to meditate and pray. They do not see through the eyes of others. Spiritual people see life through the spirit. These individuals look for opportunities to increase their spiritual awareness. They know there is something more than this physical world and refuse to limit themselves to a physical reality. This is key to their success.

Learning to Trust God within You

When problems come in life, it is an opportunity for you to trust God. One day, I received a very high electric bill in the mail that I could not afford to pay. To make matters worse, a foreclosure letter was staring me in the face. I had just had a beautiful new baby and I was suffering from preeclampsia, which is a potentially dangerous pregnancy condition associated with high blood pressure. I was unemployed and my significant other was on a drug mission. Raising four children alone and suffering post-operative pains from a c-section and toxemia were very difficult for me.

Problems seemed to come one after the next. Not knowing what to do, I began to meditate and pray, asking God to please help me. The small still voice told me to trust him. Trust? I had so many problems that trusting wasn't really on my mind. I thought that someone was playing mind games with me. Hearing voices in the face of tribulations was both assuring and confusing at the same time. I didn't realize then that problems allow for God's opportunities. As hard as things appeared, I willed my life over to God and trusted him fully.

If I decided to worry, doubt, or complain, it wouldn't have solved my problems. So, I chose to trust. A few days later a check from the Internal Revenue Service came in the mail that covered all the bills. I was not expecting any money from the IRS and neither did I remember them owing me anything. Now I understand that situation spiritually. It was God's way of turning my problem into a promise. I learned to trust the voice, the God within me. You cannot do it on your own.

"Blessed are the poor in spirit, for theirs is the kingdom of heaven. So, you and I come to a time when we stop playing games and putting on false fronts. We reach a point in life when we know we are spiritually bankrupt. It is at this point that we kneel before our Lord and say, "God I want to be born again. I want a new life. Oh God, I turn my life over to you." (Schuller, 1985)

You may not always understand why God directs you on a certain path, but if you are willing to obey him and learn his ways, you will gain insight into his heart. Don't blame your parents, your school, society's challenges, or the trials and tribulations in life. Begin to see your problems as a gateway to knowledge. Your problems are opportunities to learn about who you really are and what you are made of.

You are the Sum of Your Thoughts

You did not come to earth to suffer. In many ways, humans cause suffering. Sometimes we bring suffering on ourselves. Suffering comes primarily from your thought processes. If you think impoverished thoughts, then you will begin to feel poor, and consequently you will experience poverty. On the other hand, if you think rich, you will begin to create a world of riches all around you and you begin living life without want, lacking nothing. The universe always rewards you according to your thoughts. That is universal law. If you have negative thoughts, you are putting negative energy into the universe and will receive negative results. If you think positive the universe will give you positive results. Napoleon Hill said that one's thoughts must be mixed with emotions in order to translate them into their physical equivalent. Hill realized that you are the sum of your thoughts.

> Your problems are opportunities to learn about who you really are and what you are made of

Hill notes, "There are seven major positive emotions and seven major negative emotions." It is important for you to know the positive and negative emotions so that you can draw upon the positives and avoid the negatives.

Napoleon Hill 7 major positive emotions:

1. The emotion of Desire
2. The emotion of Faith
3. The emotion of Love
4. The emotion of Sex
5. The emotion of Enthusiasm
6. The emotion of Romance
7. The emotion of Hope

Napoleon Hill's 7 major negative emotions:

1. The emotion of Fear
2. The emotion of Jealousy
3. The emotion of Hatred
4. The emotion of Revenge
5. The emotion of Greed
6. The emotion of Superstition
7. The emotion of Anger

Make it your personal practice to mix positive thinking and positive emotions into your daily habits. Continue to seek God for inner strength. The inner strength will allow you to think optimistically, always seeing life through a positive lens. By looking through this lens you will always see positive results. Start looking for the bright side of every situation. If you know "who you are" then you will take on the future as a challenge and not as an obstacle. And when in doubt about the journey or the path, remember to always look within, search the soul. For there lies the answers.

CHAPTER FIVE

Who are You?

"It is wiser to love who you are than what you want."

—*Rasheed Ogunlaru*

To tap into your success, you must have a sense of who you are. Napoleon Hill stated, "Your business in life is, presumably, to achieve success. To be successfulyou must find peace of mind, acquire the material needs and ,above all, attain HAPPINESS. These evidences of success all begin in the forming of thought impulses." Successful people know "who they are." They know what is important in life and how to set their priorities. They respect themselves and others. Successful people don't settle for less, they constantly seek information that can help them change into more productive people.

Truly successful people do not make others feel less than great. They use their thoughts and creative energies to empower people to be their best in life.

Successful people are clear on what they want from life. These individuals live each day as if it were their last, doing at least one thing each day that will bring them closer to accomplishing one of their goals. Many successful people enjoy cultural, artistic and recreational activities. They are often spontaneous in their desires yet at the same time they are rational and mature thinkers. Life for them is a constant process of growth and change. They are intentional on self-discovery, as knowing self helps them to define their life passions.

Successful people believe in recreating themselves. Recreating oneself requires knowledge about human development. In understanding human development and behavior, you will increase knowledge about yourself. Many psychosocial experts believe that most human behaviors can be viewed by analyzing the underlying structure of each stage of development. Erik Erikson (1902 – 1994), a developmental psychologist, developed eight psychosocial stages that humans develop throughout their life span. Newman and Newman (1995) noted that the psychosocial theory represents human development as a product of the interaction between the individual (psycho) needs, and abilities and societal (social) expectations and demands.

> Life for them is a constant process of growth and change

Erikson's psychosocial development theory suggested that humans would pass through these stages from infancy to late adulthood. With every stage, the individual experiences new challenges. The individual must master functions of biological, psychological, and societal forces. According to Erickson, normal crisis distinguishes each stage. If you do not successfully resolve the normal crisis, you will carry it through to the next stage.. In other words, you will be stuck in that stage. For example: If an infant is not loved and fed often by their mother or care provider, they will experience a delay in overall growth and development.

The infant may feel abandoned internally because the infant relies on the nurturing care of their provider to receive their basic needs of comfort and security. If left forsaken, the infant may develop a distrust for people and lack personal confidence. They may also live with fear and become withdrawn. This will cause the infant to carry delayed developmental behavior into his or her next life stage. On the other hand, if a mother is consistent in providing the infant with their basic needs such as feeding him in a timely manner, changing his diaper, cuddling, and loving him, then the parent has helped to instill a sense of trust in the infant.

The trusting infant feels securely attached to his care provider. Consequently, the infant will carry the normal development of trust into his or her next stage of development. The psychosocial development theory is a phenomenon. It will help you to understand the complexity of your development at each stage of your life. The eight stages of psychosocial development shows the positive and negative resolutions that contribute to each development stage.

The eight stages of psychosocial development will bring new data to your consciousness about the patterns of development from infancy to your current age. The data will help you analyze and discover your own development that can help you to make a conscious decision to change, to move yourself forward and to become a fully functional person. The theory helps us to understand how to chart our own patterns of development. Table 1 is a chart Erikson developed to show the eight stages of psychosocial development.

TABLE 1. EIGHT STAGES OF PSYCHSOCIAL DEVELOPMENT

Age	Developmental Stage	Normal Task	Delayed Task
Infancy Birth to 2 years	Trust vs. Mistrust	Sense of basic trust	Infant is suspicious, fearful, withdrawn, physically not thriving
2 – 4 Years Toddler Hood	Autonomy vs. Shame and Doubt	Sense of control over self and personal environment	Child is obsessive, rigid, self-doubting
4 – 6 Years Early School Age	Initiative vs. Guilt	Imaginative, goal directed	Child appears guilty, suspicious, lacks spontaneity and ability to socialize
6 – 12 Years Middle School	Industry vs. Inferiority	Sense of duty and accomplishment competence	Child withdraws from peers, initial school problems

Age/Stage	Crisis	Positive Outcome	Negative Outcome
12-18 Years Early Adolescence	Identity vs. Role Confusion	Feelings of belonging, sense of purpose, goal-directed	Inability to fit in with peer group, overly self-conscious, confused with identity
18-22 Late Adolescence	Individual Identity vs. Identity Confusion	Establish identity, identity foreclosure	Negative identity
Early Adulthood 22-24 Years	Intimacy vs. Isolation	Establishment of personal significant relationship	Lack of significant relationship, strong tendency to avoid intimacy
Middle Adulthood 34-60 Years	Generativity vs. Stagnation	Positive work, caring for individuals, promoting the well-being of the next generation, concern for what is good for the next generation and achievements	Poor vocational and interpersonal achievement
Later Adulthood 60-75	Integrity vs. Despair	Promotion of intellectual vigor, acceptance of one's life	Despair, depression

Take time to study the stages of psychosocial development. Awareness of the significance of development in behaviors will help you to understand the positive and negative outcomes in each stage and to put the events of your life in perspective. Use it as a guide for self-improvement. You may find peace of mind. The psychosocial theory teaches that human development has stages from infancy to late adulthood. In each stage, there are some internal developments that take place physically, emotionally, psychologically, cognitively and socially. Table 1 describes the psychological development. When you learn to analyze your own development and behaviors you will see whether you "got stuck" or if you have developed normally.

Early memories become vehicles that carry implications between those early memories and your current condition. In my late thirties, I analyzed myself when I was attending graduate school. During my psychology course, I became conscious of my academic struggles. Reflecting on my early memories, I remembered that I got stuck at age 7, the (industry vs. inferiority) development stage. I remembered that my parents had moved to a new apartment because my brother was just born and we were living in an overcrowded, two-bedroom apartment. My parent's occupied one bedroom and my sister and I were in the other bedroom.

When we moved into the new apartment my parents had transferred me to a new school. The first school that I attended, I was in a gifted and talented program. As I reflected, I remembered the children in my class were well-behaved. I do not remember any bad experiences. However, when I attended the new school, there was no gifted and talented program and the children in my class behaved poorly. Although my parents placed me in the top

> Giving meaning to my experiences, helped me to accept my past, and make conscious decisions to change

of my 2nd grade class, I was often bullied. I began to withdraw and shy away from my peers. The problems with school began.

I started to become disruptive in class. I fought off the bullies and refused to do my class work. Without permission, I would often talk in class. When I was in the 4th grade, I failed in my academics and continued to display disruptive behaviors that caused me to repeat the same grade. The feeling of being stuck was ever-present. It wasn't until I learned about psychosocial theory in college that I was able to identify my problem and address it. My journey and my perceptions of those childhood experiences were carefully written down in my journal.

Each experience I compared with the current struggles I had in college and the struggles of deciding what I wanted to become in life. As I wrote down my perceptions and views of how I saw myself, I began to make meaning of all my experiences. Giving meaning to my experiences helped me to accept my past, and make conscious decisions to change. As a result, I began to develop and grow. My healing process began; psychologically and emotionally. With that, I began to see remarkable improvement in my academics, particularly in graduate school, graduating with a Master's degree.

Here are some step-by-step techniques that will help you to learn about your own psychological development and behavior. Be sure that you carefully analyze past experiences to chart your growth process.

Step 1: Meditation – Meditation is a practice which builds your internal self. Meditation facilitates a deep state of relaxation and eliminates any disturbing thoughts, reduces stress and restores your psychological well-being. Meditation is an excellent technique that helps to clear the mind.

To start, go to a quiet location free of disturbances. Soft music may be used if you prefer. Find a comfortable position either lying down or sitting upright. Now close your eyes. Breathe in slowly from your nostrils counting to 10 then breathe out with your mouth. Practice this for approximately 15 minutes. Now, keep your eyes closed and take your mind back to your childhood. Early memories are vehicles that are carried throughout each stage of your life. After your meditation process, write down your memories. If the memories come slowly, just be patient, they will come. Allow the memories to flow, both good and bad.

Feel the joy of the good experiences and the pain of the bad. Take some time to analyze them. What stands out most clearly in your memory? How did you feel? Why did you feel that way? If you could change your memory, to make it better, what would you have done differently and why? This will help you to make new meanings of your experiences. It will transform unhealthy memories into healthier thoughts. Now, read what you journaled. Meditate on those memories and welcome your childhood experiences. The good experiences provide

> Meditation is an excellent technique that helps to clear the mind

positive energy, whereas the bad experiences may provide negative energy.

Remember that the bad experiences still are a part of life. Allow yourself to forgive and be forgiven. My husband often says, if you don't forgive, you "keep yourself hostage." It is a universal law to forgive as forgiveness releases and heals the spirit. It will transform your mind from negative to positive. Learn to let go of all the bad experiences, forgive the person(s) who has hurt you or the situations that may have caused harmed. Release the negative energies and transform your life. Repeat this step as many times as you need to allow it to resonate within.

Step 2: Erickson believed that the adolescent matures mentally as well as physiologically. In the adolescence stage we develop new emotions, our bodies are changing, and we begin to look at life and think of the world differently from our previous stage. At the adolescence stage there are two distinct periods of psychosocial development. You can either develop a positive identity role or a role of confusion. Role confusion is the negative period. It is important that you examine this stage, it will help you to learn about yourself as an individual, a daughter/son, a student, a sister/brother, friend and so on. It will show you how the past roles and experiences are related to your present self.

This can be a difficult stage for some people as teens often struggle with a sense of identity and social issues. You may have been influenced more by your peer group to smoke cigarettes, drink alcohol, use drugs, have unprotected sex, or commit a crime. You may have had a strong drive to become popular within a negative group. On the other hand, you might have had peers that were positive and they influenced you to get good grades or to join a sports group or club.

Now close your eyes. Breathe in slowly from your nostrils counting to 10 then breathe out with your mouth. Practice this for approximately 15 minutes. Now, keep your eyes closed and take your mind back to your adolescence stage. As a frame of reference, adolescence stage is roughly the ages of 12 to 22. Whatever your experiences were, reflect on them to see how those experiences influenced you emotionally, psychologically, and socially. Write down everything that comes to your mind. Now that you have reflected on your adolescent experiences, begin to accept them. Use the power of intention in moving forward to the next stage of your life.

Step 3: The outcomes for the next process will be largely determined by your age. Whether you are in early or late adulthood reflect on whether you see yourself as stable or unstable. Do you welcome responsibility? How are your interpersonal relationships with family members, intimate partners, and colleagues? Look at those relationships. Determine the strengths and weaknesses in each relationship. Write down your discoveries in your journal.

Reflect on your journal entries and begin to access the things that you may need to improve. Your input will help you to begin creating the life that you desire and deserve.

It will help you to understand who you are. It will also help you to confront and conquer negative behavior patterns such as arguing, fighting, and living in constant conflict with others. Although change comes with difficulty for some, change can happen in an instant if you allow it to. Making the right change has everything to do with unlearning learned behaviors. Once you unlearn self-defeating behaviors, you must replace them with new knowledge and behavior that supports where you desire to go and what you want to become in life. If you believe it will work for you, it will. To become your "desired self" is a continual process of re-examination. Practicing self-examination and unlearning certain behaviors will increase your capacity for positive development.

> If you believe it will work for you, it will

Understanding the developmental stages will teach you how each stage provides a new dimension and new behavior patterns. You will discover what you have learned as a child, and experienced as an adolescent and how those patterns of development you have brought into your adulthood. As Dr. Buscagila (1978) states; "to be fully functioning, then we must be welcoming of the new as we are comfortable with the old as fearless of the unexpected as we are falsely secure in the planned." If you want to be a fully functioning person you must open your mind and spirit to accept your past, make new meaning out of it, and replace old unfruitful thoughts with new positive ones. Embrace new experiences with confidence. The future is in your hands.

DR. DIANE DAVIS PH.D.

Success is knowing oneself
It is being
"who you are"
Success is a life time journey of self-discovery.

CHAPTER SIX

Tradition

"IWhen a tradition gathers enough strength to go on for centuries, you don't just turn it off one day."
—*Chinua Achebe*

You are a unique individual. There is no one on planet earth quite like you. King David once said: "I will praise You, for I am fearfully and wonderfully made; Marvelous are Your works, And *that* my soul knows very well." Psalms 139:14. You have distinctive characteristics which set you apart from everyone else. Despite having different qualities, many of us continue to practice a way of life that our families lived many years ago. This is because we try our best to uphold tradition. Tradition is not necessarily a bad thing, but it can be a limitation to your success if you allow it.

Let's examine tradition. Tradition is a cultural pattern of beliefs, thoughts, behaviors and actions that is handed down from one generation to the next. The beliefs and values that you are taught by your parents or care providers set the foundation for your belief system. Tradition influences the same or similar behaviors and actions of your relatives. Who you are has been determined largely by your family traditions and models within the communities you live in. Some criminals come from bad communities and associate themselves with negative role models. According to Albert Bandura's Social Learning Theory, "psychological functioning is a constant shared interaction between personal, behavioral, and environmental determinants" (p. 194).

> Tradition is not necessarily a bad thing but it can be a limitation to your success if you allow it

Are You the Product of Your Tradition?

From a social learning perspective, psychological factors (thoughts and/or emotions) that are integrated both personally and environmentally provide a picture of behavior, resulting from surrounding influences. In a famous study, Bandura, Ross and Ross (1961) examined how children imitate behavior. In the study, there were two groups. The children's ages were 37 to 39 months. One group of children was exposed to an adult role model who demonstrated aggressive behavior. The second group was exposed to a non-aggressive adult model. The data indicated that children began to demonstrate many of the behaviors they observed.

Children in one group observed the adult model using physically violent behaviors and verbal aggressiveness with a Bobo doll. The children in this group repeated the same aggression toward the doll that they had observed. In the other group, most of the children exhibited non-aggressive behavior of the adult model they had observed. The findings from this study substantiated that children exposed to adult models imitated the behaviors observed in their daily lives. The conclusion of this study was that adult role models in a child's environment help shape their behavior. Simply put, we are products of our environments.

The common behaviors and actions we see in our daily life from our family, peers or people living in our communities ultimately influence our behaviors. The cultural patterns of beliefs systems that have been passed down to you from family and friends have made your life both richer and more complicated. Rollo May, an existential psychologist, noted that in our world conformity is the great destroyer of selfhood. Many people conform to the same thinking and behaviors of their parents, grandparents, and other relatives that have become socially accepted within their familial sphere. Those behaviors may be socially accepted within that family setting but not necessarily in society.

> We are products of our environments

Impoverishment of environmental stimulation in the family unit can cause an impairment of psychological functioning and developmental problems. While one family may seem to be able to handle such deprivation, the same circumstances can be psychologically detrimental to another. For example, I know of families where most of its members are quite religious. They attend church regularly. Many of them are church leaders, others very active in the ongoing functions of the church. Yet, I've seen situations where traditions allow for people to be verbally abusive to one another, unloving, and intentionally trying to destroy each other's character.

> Conformity is the great destroyer of selfhood

Not only is that behavior inappropriate, it also causes psychological damage to any person who endorses such behavior. For those that are "in the family" the abusiveness seems completely normal since abuse has become an archived element—tradition. But the larger point is that tradition doesn't necessarily have to be right. Since success has much to do with habits, you must analyze your environment to discover what traditions and habits have shaped the way you think, feel, behave, and react.

What was your relationship like with your mother or father? How did their style of rearing affect your present choices in life? In what ways do you see yourself either regressing or moving forward because of the tradition model that you were exposed to? Reflect on how that makes you feel? After

> The larger point is that tradition doesn't necessarily have to be right

pondering these questions, you will begin to reflect on how conforming to certain traditions may have lent to the destruction of your selfhood and ultimately to the demise of your success.

Repeating and Reliving Your Past

To better understand this philosophy, it is necessary that you understand the source and nature of the conflict that tradition continues to play in your life. You must develop the courage to confront cycles of tradition that directly oppose where you desire to be in life. As a graduate student, I interned as a counselor at a homeless shelter. I focused on how tradition played an integral role in the life of my counseling studies. Many of the parents I counseled revealed that they parented much like their parents. If their parents were physically and mentally abusive, they too found themselves demonstrating the same behavior toward their children.

Those who I counseled admitted that they were abused and neglected by their parents and repeated the same behavior with their children. Through counseling sessions, my clients were able to explore and understand their current parental styles and how it affected their children's lives. Although, most of the parents "got stuck" in their traditional situation, they

> Tradition often seems too large to confront or overcome for most people, so they just accept it as normal

could identify with their past, present and future behaviors. Eventually most of them were able to examine their family's tradition, how it affected them, and then confront them to create lasting change. I carefully observed and listened and at first sensed feelings of hopelessness. They seemed hopeless in that tradition often seems too large to confront or overcome for most people, so they just accept it as normal.

From my research and private sessions, I discovered that individual behavior is adopted or established tgriugh family tradition or exposure to communal environments. Most of the parents that I counseled were surprised to realize that they were repeating the identical behavior patterns of their parents or care providers. Until you take time to analyze and understand your tradition, you may never realize how deeply it impacts you and everything you do. These factors determine your beliefs, values, religion, spirituality and social behaviors. It develops personality, emotional qualities, and behavioral patterns.

When you begin to understand the way in which tradition plays a role from birth throughout your adult life, you will get a better grip on your life now, and what exactly brought you to this point. Your willingness to access this area of your life will help to move closer to your understanding of how you allowed tradition to destroy your selfhood, and what you may do to initiate the process back to recovery of the real you. Many experts state that to become a psychologically healthy person, several stages of consciousness of one's self are needed. Rediscovery of self is a very important stage in becoming successful.

You must face each stage of development and break the imaginary umbilical cord in exchange for your independence. When I view society as a system, I view the families as subsystems interacting to make the society function. How each individual and their family behaves affects what happens in society. For example, a person who has grown up in Spanish Harlem and has never ventured away from their neighborhood may be inclined to mirror all the values of a Caribbean, Central or South American country, thousands of miles away. The challenge to become "different than" is heightened by tradition and culture.

Tradition and culture are not negative things in and of themselves. However, tradition can be a limitation to forward progression in a new world. Some first-generation immigrant Hispanic parents are faced with the challenging task of parenting their children within an American culture with completely different traditions. The parents' loyalty to their native country at times forces them to enforce traditional behaviors that become normal to their offspring. Yet, when these children attend local public schools they are presented with the task of becoming socialized into the American culture or, as some see it, the "culture of what's cool."

The doors to success are always plural. There are many doors. But just as there are many doors, there are many blockages if we do not see them. Tradition can be a good thing. But at times it can also be a blockage to your success in life. Being wholeheartedly committed to your parents or grandparents' vision may not work for you. There is a difference between respecting your forefather, which I wholeheartedly believe in, and following one's own path. Following your own path in life is necessary to becoming successful. But in order to successfully follow your own path, you must be willing to submit to taking a look at yourself—self-analysis.

Napoleon Hill states that, "self-analysis may disclose your weaknesses that you do not acknowledge." He further noted that, "it is your own responsibility to face the facts directly and to ask yourself crystal clear questions and demand direct replies". It is only when you become aware of your traditions and customs and how they play a role in your behavior and in society that you can change your outcome. Remember the first step is in being aware. Become aware and take full responsibility to learn where your behaviors stem from and make a conscious decision to change your actions from negative to positive. Only keep and hold dear those traditions that continue to serve you. Discard the ones that no longer serve you as they inhibit your growth and progress in life.

> Only keep and hold dear, the traditions that continue to serve you. Discard the ones that no longer serve you as they inhibit your growth and progress in life

You must have faith in your unique self to break tradition that block you from achieving your goals

CHAPTER SEVEN

Tradition

"Faith is taking the first step even when you don't see the whole staircase."
—*Martin Luther King*

Faith is believing in things unseen, but hoped for. The Bible teaches Christians to "walk by faith not by site" (2 Corinthians 5:7). Faith is an unwavering system of belief. It is having confidence, trust and assurance without manifested proof. Faith is having initial expectations in your mind before it becomes your reality. My expectation is that this book will help to build your belief that your dreams and desires will become your reality. Because I wrote the book, that put my faith into action. Genuine faith never exists alone. It must be accompanied by corresponding actions.

If you are in a state of discouragement, feeling powerless or having no hope for your future, you are putting negative energy into the universe and you will not achieve your desired outcome. If you believe, have confidence, hope, and trust in a power greater than yourself then you can achieve! Acting right now will help you begin to build your faith, hope, expectations and a brighter future. Practice faith by focusing your attention on the spirit of God. The spirit of God will give you knowledge, wisdom and understanding.

> Faith is having initial expectations in your mind before it becomes your reality

The Spirit of the LORD shall rest upon Him, The Spirit of wisdom and understanding, The Spirit of counsel and might, The Spirit of knowledge and of the fear of the LORD.
Isaiah 11:2

Webster's New World Dictionary defines faith as an unquestioning belief that does not require proof or evidence. It also calls faith an unquestioning belief in God. If you have a faith deficiency, it is impossible for the universe to bring the desire that you are seeking. Lack of faith will not inspire any good actions. If you believe without having proof you will achieve your desire, because you placed confidence in the God within you to bring things to past. If you had the proof, then you really wouldn't need faith. Faith is only for those who have nothing to prove but everything to gain.

> Faith is only for those who have nothing to prove but everything to gain

Fear is the Opposite of Faith

Faith provides you with limitless resources. Always write down what you are striving for. Always put a date on when you expect it. Whenever you reach an objective, check it off your list. Celebrate every objective that you achieve. The celebration will remind you that you've not only stood the test but that you also confronted your fears and won. There is no problem that faith cannot address. It doesn't matter how large or small the problem is, faith can fix it. One of the qualities of some of the most successful people on the planet is that they choose to live in faith with regards to their goals.

They realize that living in fear paralyzes their blessing and eliminates their reward. Fear is faith on the other end of the coin. It takes as much energy to not believe as it does to believe. The choice is yours as to which side you want to live on. Don't live in fear. Fear is the opposite of faith, and fear always produces opposite and unfavorable results. Some time ago my dear friends, the Browns, had an issue with their son and his elementary school in New York City that only faith could fix. Sallie and Tom Brown understood and practiced good parenting skills.

They had high values and lived by ethical principles in front of their son. However, Sallie and Tom were faced with a crisis and

> It takes as much energy to not believe as it does to believe. The choice is yours as to which side you want to live on

did not know exactly what to do. Their son's fifth grade teacher was abusing him both mentally and verbally. The teacher was speaking to him in an inappropriate and condescending manner. And the abusiveness began to take a toll on their son. The Browns were upset about the abusive situation, yet had no real solutions. They requested to meet with me for a family counseling session. During the session, we discussed the problem and I offered various approaches to addressing it.

The Browns trusted in the plan that I gave them, but had to "act" in courage to confront the teacher and administrators about what was going on. Some parents do not realize that they have rights when it comes to large systems such as the public education system. Some parents view systems as large, insensitive, and above the law. With that, many parents may refrain from confronting certain situations, believing that their voice won't be heard. I encouraged them to walk in faith and believe for a favorable outcome. They agreed to confront the matter, but requested my presence at the meeting.

To cover all bases, I suggested that the Browns meet with their son's teacher, various students involved, school administrators, and the community school board concerning this issue. We all met on the matter and one of the school board members was there as well. The meeting went well and the Browns were satisfied with the end results. The next day, after that conference, the Browns' son went to school and experienced a positive change from his teachers and other school officials. He began to get enthusiastic about going to school. His teacher began treating him better as her attitude and approach totally improved.

There are some that do not realize just how damaging verbal, mental or even spiritual abusiveness can be. If not confronted and dealt with early on, it can have drastic negative effects on a child's development, following them into adulthood. The Browns' faith yielded them the results of having a healthily developed child. You may be a parent or know of a parent who is experiencing a similar challenge. The point is not to act, react, or become paralyzed with fear as that only produces negative outcomes.

Going into the meeting the Browns had no proof of what was going to happen. There were no guarantees that the teacher wouldn't have lashed out defensively concerning the matter. The only real thing that the Browns had to hold onto was their faith, their faith that everything was going to be alright.

> Faith is not merely a feel-good word, but rather the daily lifestyle of the truly successful

They went in not having proof, but having hope that they would receive a favorable solution for their son's problem.

No matter what you desire to do, be or become, no matter how big the problems are in your life right now, you will get through it with faith. Fear always causes motion in the wrong direction. Faith always drives you toward the solutions in life. Stay in faith and continue to realize that faith is not merely a feel-good word, but rather the daily lifestyle of the truly successful.

"Faith is having an initial expectation in your mind.

It's believing in things unseen, but hoped for.

It's having confidence and trust in a power greater than yourself."

CHAPTER EIGHT

Reading Is Still Fundamental

"Without question reading has been the foundation of whatever success I've had in my life."
—Hugh McColl Jr. –former Chairman and CEO Bank of America

Take time to read every day. Reading is a fundamental step to success. It can provide the basis and foundation, procedures, and processes needed to secure a better future. One person once said, "anything you want to know is written in a book." In our inter-networked, inter-connected society, it can be safely said that even if it's not in book, you can get valuable information online via your computer, your phone, or a tablet. Reading can help shed light on anything you're confused about. It can improve your perception. Reading can help you to meet your needs and help you to meet the needs of others around you.

If you are in a state of discouragement, or feeling powerless, the earth is replete with knowledge and information. By reading books, magazines, journals or newspapers you can learn something new that may be your personal turning point in life. If you are serious about change you must understand that lasting change is always preceded by practicing principles, techniques, theories and laws. Many of these can be found in writing. You don't have to reinvent the wheel in life. All you have to do is follow the example of those that have already done what you desire to do. Read and take the shorter path by learning from other's examples.

Reading is much like having an internal navigational system that guides you safely to your destination. My advice to people who desire to know more about the how tos of business is to find some books written by successful business leaders and read them. Most good business books lay out the plan and procedures on how to do what they did. Many business people who write books are often transparent about their triumphs and their struggles. They will tell you about the pitfalls that almost cost them their business, families, and lives and how you can avoid those pitfalls alltogether.

Stimulate your thinking and increase your knowledge. There are no rockets to success. You'll have to take the road like everyone else. To get great results, you must apply yourself to study, and apply what you've learned. Reading will give you the insights as well as the practical information you need to start or restart your journey to success. When someone gives you a book as a gift, it's far more than a gift, it's an act of love. It is an act of love in that they are giving you something that has the capacity to usher lasting change in your life, if you utilize it.

When I decided to make a major change in my life, I began to read spiritual self-help books, including the Bible. The spiritual information in the books helped to shape a more positive outlook on life. The trials and tribulations that I was going through were much easier to deal with, understanding that the tests of life do not last forever. It was also during this time, that I was emotionally unstable. I was dealing with a violent husband who abused me physically and emotionally. My emotions were completely out of control because I didn't understand why this was happening to me.

> When someone gives you a book as a gift, it's far more than a gift, it's an act of love

Deep inside of my spirit I was crying out for help. Little did I know that a large part of my help would come as I began to read. A stranger on the street gave me a Bible and began reading it. The words in that book began to minster life to me. I began to get a second wind and a new lease on life. I became so excited that I wanted to read everything I could get my hands on. I didn't have a lot of money back then, so I visited the local library and checked out as many books as they would allow me to.

There was a wealth of books to read in the library. My mind began to open to gain new understanding that produced actions. A whole new world was unlocked. All the areas in life that had previously challenged me, I began to read the solutions for these problems in books.

I'd read everything; books on domestic violence, personal finance, how to raise children effectively, and how to be happy in life. It was through reading spiritual books that I developed a personal relationship with God, one of which I am proud to own and share with anyone willing to listen. Reading created positive change in my life, which is why I am a lifelong reader.

Wholeheartedly I believe that God uses authors on this earth to communicate messages that he wants us to know to help us along our journey. I've heard some people say that they don't really like to read, or that reading takes too long, or that it's boring. The truth is reading is therapeutic. Reading is also the perfect me-time activity guaranteed to shift you into another level of consciousness. Take it slow. Do it at your own pace. Expect amazing results.

> Reading created positive change in my life, which is why I am a lifelong reader

It is chiefly through books that we enjoy intercourse with superior minds. In the best books, great men talk to us, give us their most precious thoughts and pour their souls into ours. God we thank you for books. They are the voices of the distant and the dead, and make us heirs of the spiritual life of past ages. Books are true levelers. They give to all who will faithfully use them, the society, the spiritual presence, of the best and greatest of our race.

~ William Ellery Channing

CHAPTER NINE

VISION

"The most pathetic person in the world is some one who has sight but no vision."
—*Helen Keller*

Vision is ingenious. It is a source of power. With a vision, you possess great mental abilities and skills to fuel your ideas. You see things in your imagination before it exists in manifested form. Ask yourself, what do I want to create? When you close your eyes, you can visualize in your mind's eye everything that you desire. You see it in your mind because its real. What kind of house do you want to live in? How much money do you want your business to earn this year? Who is your target market and how can you serve them better? What have you desired to create in life? These things are the products of your vision.

Without your vision, nothing will ever become a reality. You should visualize your ideals both morning and evening each day. Your vision is a mental imagery of what you long for. Interestingly, there are some ministers and prophets on the earth who are known as visionaries because they have a God-given ability to see what will come before it happens.

> Without your vision, nothing will ever become a reality

Although there are certain people who are spiritually gifted in a unique way, we all have the capacity to see visions. Vision sends signals from the subconscious mind into the universe and connects you with your desired goal. Vision provides subliminal thoughts into the universe and creates a renewed reality.

In 1982, I had a vision to found a community-based social service agency to foster community stabilization and to provide programs for children, adolescents, seniors, low-income single mothers and families. My vision was clear. I saw the office five years before actually renting the commercial space and the facilities where the youth programs took place. A small group of community residents met with me one day at my apartment to discuss community needs and new program intervention strategies that would help improve the community. Five years after initially receiving my vision, the state of New York issued us a certificate of incorporation and our community-based organization was established.

Before my vision came into fruition, I shared my vision with people in the community. Many of the residents and leaders shared my vision with others, which was to uplift the quality of life for children and their families. At that time, there were no organized, structured programs for children and adolescents in the urban community in New York City. Many of the locally elected officials were concerned about the rise of drug use, crime, and the high school dropout rate. These problems made it easier for elected officials to fund organizations that would address and help solve the problems.

Within months of obtaining the certificate of incorporation the organization had raised more than $800,000 dollars, making it necessary to lease an office, hire staff and expand our programming. After three years had passed, I experienced extraordinary growth and the organization had become the central organization where people in this community were receiving support and social services. We were honored by The New York Women's Foundation. We received city and state awards. Because I cast my vision forth and mixed it with faith, the organization became a reality and helps many people today. I know firsthand that you can begin with a seed called vision and when watered, it will become a reality.

When the organization was formed, I had no formal instruction on how to operate this business. I knew nothing about the rules of properly leading a non-profit organization. Looking back, I now believe that I didn't need to know those things at all. What I needed was vision. And I had that. It was vision that continued to lead me to each stage. Vision inspired me to seek out the knowledge on how to successfully lead an organization of this type. We were providing jobs to the residents as our vision expanded. That's when I fully realized that vision is not only about you, vision is about those you are called to influence and serve.

Your subconscious mind is the seedbed where many visions, dreams, desires, and hopes are germinated. There is no hope for you if you do not have a vision. Without a vision, you have no mental imagery to create a plan for your future. Vision leads you to the place that you want to be. Many children I've counseled had a vision to become a teacher, accountant, business owner or a professional basketball player. After reviewing their progress after a decade, all of them are now young adults and they are living out exactly what they desired. Their vision brought them to the place they dreamed of being.

See Like a Child

> *And he said: "Truly I tell you, unless you change and become like little children, you will never enter the kingdom of heaven. Matthew 18:3 (NIV)*

As a child, do you remember daydreaming or imagining what your life would be like when you grew up? Well, guess what? Many successful people are living the dream that they once visualized in their subconscious mind as children. A close friend of mine wanted to be a millionaire. She

> Vision is not only about you, vision is about those you are called to influence and serve

shared with me her dreams of how her lifestyle would be in the future. My friend believed that her dream of millionaire status would one day become a reality. She held that belief in her subconscious mind and would not let it go. Today, she is a millionaire. She left New York, moved to Florida and is now living out the life she visualized.

When it comes to vision you won't always know the exact road to take or the moves to make. Don't worry. Vision evolves and unfolds. A friend always reminds me that "whatever God has for you, you will have it. And no man can take it from you, but you." The important thing is that you take the quality time to meditate and hold fast within your subconscious the vision that you have until it appears in the physical form. Listen to the voice within to give directions.

Vision attracts vision and visionaries. Like attracts like. Successful people visualize themselves socializing with other successful people. Whatever you envision for yourself, associate with people who are living your vision. Choose friends that support your vision and those who are living the life that you dream of. You are the company that you keep. Visionaries produce and inspire others to become visionaries.

> *As cited by Carson (1992):*
> *"You become like the people you spend your time with. You have to be careful in selecting friends. Sometimes people think they can hang out with a certain crowd and are sure they won't become like them. They think that somehow they are immune from the influence. But they're only*

fooling themselves.

After a while they begin to act like them and absorb aspects of their personality without noticing it. Before long they start becoming the same kind of individual as those they hang out with."

Whatever you admire in that person or group of people is a good reason to surround yourself with them. The good qualities that you observe in them will eventually rub off on you. Make this confession, "Today, I make a conscious decision to socialize with friends with which I have similar interests and values. My friends are empathetic, caring and understanding individuals." When I make my confessions I add: "We spend our leisure time at Broadway theaters, jazz and classical concerts, museums, restaurants and dinner parties talking about new interventions that will uplift the quality of life for all people. My inner circle is full of meaningful philanthropists. Each one of us works to enhance the well-being of humanity." Be specific in your confession. Confession brings possession.

> Be specific in your confession. Confession brings possession

When I was a child, I visualized having friends that would have similar interests and improve my social position. Today, I have amazing friends that share similar interests and provide their support and encouragement when needed. I'm living the dream. The phenomenon of surrounding yourself with people with similar interests, values and behaviors will change you for the better. My friends have helped me to be a better person, professionally and socially. Having a vision and surrounding yourself around other like-minded people will inspire new concepts and ideas that will usher you into the place where you add most value to humanity.

Vision is the source and hope of life. The greatest gift ever given to mankind is not the gift of sight, but the gift of vision. Sight is a function of the eyes; vision is a function of the heart. "Eyes that look are common, but eyes that see are rare." ~ Dr. Myles Munroe

CHAPTER TEN

MIND/THOUGHT PROCESS

"Put your heart, mind, and soul into even your smallest acts. This is the secret of success."
—*Swami Sivananda*

When you make up your mind that you want to change, change will occur. You cannot remain where you are, because there is transformative power in your mind. The mind is a collection of thoughts. Thoughts are things that produce actual results. It is important to know that everything begins with a thought. How you think will control your life. This means that you are ultimately in control of your life, since you are in control of your thoughts. There are two thought processes, rational and irrational. In the simplest form, rational is positive thinking and irrational is negative thinking.

> When you make up your mind that you want to change, change will occur

Some people have a propensity toward happiness, sadness, living rich or poor, or being immature, although they are adults. These various states are created by the mind and through thoughts. Sigmund Freud, the father of psychoanalysis viewed the mind as a complex energy system. Freud suggested that our personality is established by three elements of hypothetical structure of the mind; the id, ego and superego. The id is the first system of your personality. The id is a component of your personality that begins at birth. The id is the main source of psychic energy and primitive instinct.

The id does not tolerate tension as it immediately rids itself of tensions when it presents itself, to return to a homeostatic state. The id is driven by pleasure. If your pleasure needs and wants are not met you may suffer with anxiety or with disruptive behaviors that are not generally welcomed in society. The id is unconscious and tries to resolve tension immediately to create pleasure, which entails creating a mental image in your mind of a desired outcome.

The ego deals with reality. It is developed from the id and controls and regulates the personality. Gerald Corey, author of Theory and Practice of Counseling and Psychotherapy noted that ego is ruled by the "reality principle." The reality principle is the mind's ability to evaluate the reality of the external world and to act on it accordingly. The ego utilizes logical thinking, putting together a plan of actions to satisfy needs. The ego functions in the conscious. Your unconscious state houses past experiences, emotions and thoughts that are hidden and that may be painful to process and accept. The ego can discharge all the pain that is difficult to deal with.

The superego is the component of your personality that comprises the internalized standards of your parents and society. The superego represents traditions, morals, values, culture, and ideas about right from wrong that have been learned and passed down. Understanding these personality types can help you better understand how your mind works and how you process your thoughts. When you begin to understand how your mind works this will help you to improve areas of your life that were dormant, leading you to greater levels of success.

Train Your Brain for Positive Results

You can train your mind to have positive thoughts. Affirmations are a great way to train your mind. Affirmations are declarations that can help you develop positive thoughts. Thoughts and words have power and they influence the universe. When I was raising my children, I trained them to think positive. They were not allowed to use the word "can't." When they made mistakes, and said "can't," I explained that the word was negative and it would prevent them from reaching their full potential. If my children were performing a difficult task, I reminded them to say, "I can do it." This motivated them to continue to try until they realized their desired result.

You become whatever you dwell on. This is why meditation is so important. Your greatest gift to the universe and to others is becoming all that you can be. You were not born knowing the difference between right and wrong, it is a learned behavior. In the same way, training your thoughts is a learned behavior. Religion teaches us moral ethics and how to live righteously. Righteous living is about being moral, based on your religion's standards and interpretations of morality. Most religions aim for the same goal of living a good and ethical lifestyle, treating your fellow man with respect and honor.

However, none of their objectives come to fruition by mere chance. Their goal of indoctrination happens because they typically teach their principles and guidelines to their followers from birth. In the same way, if you focus on practicing right over wrong thinking you will become a master of your own mind and a master of yourself in time. Imagine if you practice right-thinking from birth, you will have made remarkable progress long before you've reached adulthood. Proper training produces remarkable results.

"According to the Buddhist philosophy, to improve the mind is based on interdependence. This is mainly concerned with pain and pleasure, and the fact that everything in life is interlinked creating a chain reaction. In understanding this, it will develop concern for the wider perspective. When putting this to practice we promote loving, kindness and compassion. It also reduces ones anger and hatred." (Renuka Singh, 1999)

Products of Environment or Thinking?

Many people may have been raised in disadvantaged and dysfunctional families. Some have attended failing schools and lived in deprived communities. No matter what your situation was or is, you should not allow that to define you. You should not allow those things to bring pain to you, as it is not reflective of who you are. Those things are simply conditions, conditions of the mind. The family you were born into, the neighborhood you grew up in, or the schooling you had or didn't have are all conditions.

I once worked in an educational institution where I saw school officials treating young students poorly because they had labeled and profiled them. Some of the students came from two or three generations of family dysfunction. Some of them were in and out of the social system. Because of this, these school officials did not view them as regular children. They viewed them as dysfunctional children that needed to be treated poorly. Some of their parents never graduated high school, lacked parenting skills, and allowed their children to do what they wanted to do. They weren't governed.

Some of the school officials took advantage of this because they knew that they could and get away with it. It is sad that there are people who exacerbate the problems of children instead of helping to improve them. But the larger point is not so much how the leadership mistreated the young students. The central theme is that these children could have changed their outcome if they changed their thinking. Regardless of how they were being treated, had they focused on who they could be and become, that would have changed their outcome and ultimately reversed some of the maltreatment.

Had they thought that they could possibly connect with the right people who had similar goals and objectives, then they may have had a more favorable outcome. I'm not suggesting that the maltreatment was their fault. Rather, I am suggesting that positive thoughts can reverse negative results. If they focused on the pain of their situation, they'll get more pain. If they focused on the pleasure of the possibility of their future success, they would have received more of that. Buddhist teaching says that pain and pleasure cause a chain reaction. Whatever you hold onto in your mind you will inevitably get more of. That is why it is necessary to release other people's negative energy even before it gets into you.

The author Karl Albrech (1980) of Brain Power states that "the adaptive fluent thinker enjoys mental life and finds many interesting things to do." The active thinker should never allow negative thoughts to linger. If a thought of lack comes to my mind, I immediately replace it by confessing, "God will supply all my needs, the spirit will open my mind that I may receive wisdom, knowledge and understanding to do the right thing in life, and lead me in the right path toward wealth and honor. When you replace roaming negative thoughts with positive affirmations, you immediately arrest the criminal of negative thoughts and sentence him to outer darkness.

What if My Friends Resist Me?

When you commit to change and chart a new positive path, you will always encounter initial resistance. Your change may bother your family and friends as they are accustomed to the old you and your old ways. Don't fret, because resistance to change is a normal reaction. Often, family members and friends resist change in you, because they are frightened of your success. Without you even trying, your success shines a beaming light on their failures, shortcomings, and insecurities. Your success forces them to accept the fact that they too could be successful if they changed their thoughts, their minds and their actions.

"The things which you learned and received and heard and saw in me, these you do, and the God of peace will be with you" (Philippians 4:9).

People fail to put into practice what they've learned. There is so much that we learn daily. But how much do we put it into practice? Success starts with a positive attitude. It is how you think. But you must accept that negative people will always be there. You must be sure not to give them your mind. For the most part, the negative people you encounter will be friends and family. Strangers generally do not have an impact on you the way a friend will and thus won't make a real difference in how you think. Because you care for your loved ones you also care about what they think. However,

> Resistance to change is a normal reaction

you must choose to care more about your success than the opinions of negative people.

Negative people will always move stealthily to provide you with a biased or objective opinion that does not give you the energy you need. In time, this will deplete you. They are willing and satisfied to accept the negative in their lives and expect that you should do the same. What I'd like you to realize is that negative people serve as a test to your strength. The old phrase says, "only the strong survive." The strong survive, because they know how to control their thoughts.

Even though I have enjoyed a considerable amount of success, I am still constantly confronted by negative people. I'm not immune to their persecution. Yet, I am on guard. Sometimes, they creep in (when I allow them to) and interrupt my peaceful flow. Without them realizing it, negative people's behavior affects them just as much as it does others. For example: a negative person could have feelings of jealousy for another person, trying their best to make their opponent feel bad. While they do this, they are feeling even worse in the process.

People who feel good about themselves cannot possibly get joy from making others feel bad. They do this as a cover-up to their own deteriorating state of being. Many people who live in a constant state of jealousy toward others, or who always seek to destroy other's character and reputation through spreading rumors and gossip often have an undiagnosed mental illness. Attacking someone's character is not a normal healthy-minded trait. You cannot solve their problems. But you can decrease the effects of their attack against you. You do this through meditation. Block out their attacks and focus your mind and thoughts on what you desire. That will rid you of their toxicity.

Positive thinking skills are not inherited. These skills are honed and cultivated. Oddly, there are times when difficulty and tough circumstances help to produce positive results. We tend to learn more valuable lessons from hard times than good time. An expert artist will sometimes draw a picture several times until it is exactly as she desires it to be. You must be willing to change your thoughts if you want to make change no matter how long it takes. Furthermore, you must make the quality decision to only meditate on things that bring life and value to you.

> If you don't conquer self-defeating thoughts, they will in time dominate and control your mind. Defeat any voices that oppose your dreams and desires in life

"Finally brethren, whatever things are true, whatever things are noble, whatever things are just, whatever things are pure, whatever things are lovely, whatever things are of good report, if there is any virtue and if there is anything praise worthy medtiate on these things (Philippians 8:4).

If you don't conquer self-defeating thoughts, they will in time dominate and control your mind. Defeat any voices that oppose your dreams and desires in life. Replace those voices with this affirmation. "I can and

I will start thinking positive today." Say that as often as you can all throughout your day. You will begin to see major progress in the overall process of controlling your thoughts to receive your reward of abundance.

" When we put the forces of our inner self to work with good thoughts, it will produce to our system of ideas, If we can keep our inner world clean, fertilize our minds with productive positively, the powers within will create, the dynamic force, all that we believe is possible. "

(Iyanla Vanzant, 1993)

CHAPTER ELEVEN

EXERCISE

"Pain is temporary. It may last a minute, or an hour, or a day, or a year, but eventually it will subside and something else will take its place. If I quit, however, it lasts forever."
—Lance Armstrong

It would be remiss of me if I did not emphasize the importance of exercise in the life of the truly successful. A quality exercise routine will benefit your mind, body and soul. Before any exercise program, I recommend that you get a complete physical by your doctor. Inform your doctor of your exercise goals, whether basic fitness or weight loss. A good physician will provide a guide to instruct you on methods to get the best results and be safe.

> A quality exercise routine will benefit your mind, body and soul

Exercise helps to increase your stamina and strength. It increases your energy. It heightens your enthusiasm and drive as you pursue your desires. Exercise increases brain chemicals like serotonin and dopamine. Serotonin is a neurotransmitter. It is a chemical substance that sends out nerve impulses across neurons. According to a Princeton University research study, serotonin is known as a "happiness hormone." Dopamine is also a neurotransmitter that plays several roles in the brain. It helps control the part of the brain that provides reward and pleasure systems. According to an article in Psychology Today (2014) dopamine can help regulate movement and emotional responses.

People who exercise regularly are more likely to reach their goals, attain rewards, and to consistently act on meaningful tasks. Walking, running, aerobics or any other physical exercise can give you the movement and vitality to keep you energized enough to develop a plan to help you attain your short and long-term goals. Successful people need to be in great shape to always avail themselves to opportunity. Exercise not only burns calories and helps to rid yourself of unwanted fats but, it is also helps to strengthen the heart and bones. It also increases your metabolism, which helps to properly regulate healthy weight, even when you are not exercising.

> Successful people need to be in great shape to always avail themselves to opportunity

When you increase your metabolism, you allow a chemical reaction of organisms to compel desirable response to generate energy that without rigorous movement would not occur. According to experts to get a total workout, you need to simply begin by putting one foot in front of the other. You don't have to be Arnold Schwarzenegger, just by implementing a simple walking routine you will see remarkable results in a short amount of time. Each week, I walk three days for twenty minutes alongside the Atlantic Ocean in Brooklyn, New York.

Not only does exercise help keep my stomach firm, it also releases tension and motivates me to plan and act on my dreams. There are a multitude of ways that exercise can benefit your body. There is also a body spirit connection that comes with exercise as it rejuvenates the spirit. With exercise, understand that proper breathing should be a vital part of your exercise routine. Position yourself in a comfortable position. Begin to take deep, slow breaths if you are lying down or sitting upright.

Inhale through your nose. Take in deep full breaths from your diaphragm. Exhale fully through your mouth. Once you feel your body totally relaxed, start walking slowly so that you can warm your muscles up. Do this for about five minutes then increase your speed for another five minutes. For five minutes, slow down and walk slowly to cool down. Practice these walking techniques for at least 20 minutes a day. The point is to just do something and keep moving!

"Exercise is a great way to release stress, feel good and to provide synergy to motivate you to reach your goals to make your dreams a reality."

CHAPTER TWELVE
AFTERWORD

To achieve your success in life is to understand what success means to you. Then change will happen. Success can mean anything you want it to. You assign the value to what success is or is not. If you make a mental effort to analyze yourself, develop positive thoughts, have a strong desire, a plan, and season it with faith, and execute your plan, you will achieve success. That may seem like a lot of things to do, but doing nothing will certainly yield you nothing in life. Success comes when you make certain actions a habit.

As a philosopher and a mental health counselor, I fully realize that what adds value to life is being psychologically healthy, proper development, and knowing who you are. When you recognize these things, you are inclined to live in abundance and from a place of gratefulness.

> Once you solve your problems you become an expert in that area and can charge for your counsel

When you accept all your experiences in life, the good and the bad, you can move forward. But more importantly, you will have the tools and the know-how to navigate through any storm that life brings your way. Your problems then become an actual gift. Once you solve your problems you become an expert in that area and can charge for your counsel. That will lead you to financial freedom.

Giving Back

There is no such thing as real success without sharing with others. It is to your advantage not only to make a difference in life, but also to help someone else along the way. After you have "made it" in life, give back. After you have mastered some of the techniques and teachings that I've shared with you, find ways to give back to others. Help others to become successful as well. True success is not about how much you can hoard, but rather how much you can share. How can you help to improve another person's life?

When you help others, a karmic reality is set in motion. The more you give to others, you create a space for others to always give back to you. The way to reach your goals the quickest, is to help others in their process. Never look at giving away from yourself as drudgery. Life is a win-win situation! Always remembers that. So, don't forget to help your neighbor along the way as you reach your desires. Remember, that what you make happen in another person's life will always happen for you.

Knowing When to Separate

Writing this book was cathartic for me insofar as it helped me to purge parts of my past and clarify my life's purpose. It helped to strengthen my own mind. It also helped me to recognize something that I didn't always understand, and that is that my social groups were no longer meeting my needs. I was experiencing stagnation, as I had outgrown the people in my circle. Because of my connection to certain people, I had stopped growing, since they weren't growing. Remember, you are the company that you keep. I had to make a tough but much needed choice.

I chose to separate from the social group for my internal growth and mental sanity. At that time, I also began to realize that I had outgrown my first husband. At the age of 14 we began dating. At 17 I married my first love. We stayed together for 15 years. At first things were fine, but as time went on I began to suffer with emotional problems and instability. The intimacy in our relationship had gone and I was desperately seeking ways to free myself from the struggle. One day I mustered up the courage to divorce him and was left to raise three children alone.

After the divorce, he essentially abandoned us, and never came back to visit or provide financial support. That was a problem that life dealt me. I decided to grow from that. Having to care for my children, I wanted to be an expert care provider. I didn't want my children to miss being psychologically healthy, and healthy as normal kids should be. I began taking parenting classes at a local head start program. It taught me how to raise my children more effectively. All the skills and knowledge that I had learned, I used when I founded my non-profit organization.

I began to train parents using my experiences and training as the basis for my instruction. I took a negative situation and turned it into a positive one. It began with me recognizing that it was time to separate. Had I stayed there, I may not be alive today. My children may have ended up in very bad situations. Worse yet, I would not have been able to be a blessing to the universe in the way I have been. Separating from negative and toxic people opened the floodgates to opportunities that I'd otherwise never have known.

> Separating from negative and toxic people opened the floodgates to opportunity that I'd otherwise never have known

Power in Knowledge

As we bring our journey to a temporary close, realize that this book may be coming to an end, but your life is just beginning. After that, your life will begin again and again. The point is that you will continue to be re-born as you re-educate yourself to new knowledge and new realities. Stagnation comes by exposing yourself to the same people, same situations, same environments, same neighborhoods and so on. Life becomes interesting as you aquire new knowledge. That is what I am encouraging you to stay committed to—new knowledge.

Belleruth Naparstek says that "greater access to information gives us more power, and more power always requires greater accountability and responsibility." Knowledge is power but with that power comes a sense of obligation and duty. When a person gets knowledge, they can do good or evil. The choice is theirs. Adolf Hitler was an extremely knowledgeable person who used his knowledge to destroy human life. That was the choice he made. As you receive knowledge, make a commitment to yourself that you will use your newfound knowledge to empower lives and improve the condition of life for humanity.

My objective for writing this book was not about helping you to get a bigger house or an exotic car. My objective was to help you to understand that success connects with success. Your success is directly connected to others. The world is full of need. There is the need for food, shelter, and clothing. Poverty runs deep in many countries. Starvation, lack of clean air and water are problems for many communities. Many children do not have access to quality education around the world. Disease and sickness run rampant throughout many impoverished communities. The purpose of this work is to empower you to make a difference. You can do it!

You can change the lives of many through your labor of love. You are blessed to be a blessing. Begin to view yourself differently than before. Start realizing that all your trials and struggles were for a reason.

> You are the success you've been looking for

Know that you went through hell so that you could give someone heaven. You are the difference in life that someone is seeking. Success is not a thing. It is not something you can purchase. Success is rightfully a journey. The one thing you will realize as you begin this journey is that success starts and ends with you, because you are the success you've been looking for. It is within you.

Recommended Readings

The 7 Habits of Highly Effective People: Powerful Lessons in Personal Change (1989). Stephen R. Covey

Total law of Attraction: Unleash your Secret Creative Power to Get what you want (2013). Dr. David Che

Law of Attraction (2006). Esther Hicks & Jerry Hicks

What makes the Great Great (1997) Dennis Kimbro, Ph.D.

Personhood: The Art of Being Fully Human (1978). Leo F. Buscaglia, Ph.D.

Bibliography

Albrecht, K. (1980). Brain power: Learn to improve your thinking skills. New York: Simon & Schuster.

Bandura, A. (1977). Social learning theory. Upper Saddle River, New York. Prentice Hall.

Bandura, A., Ross, D., & S.A. (1961). Transmission of aggression through imitation of aggressive models. Journal of Abnormal and Social Psychology, 63, 575-582. Doi:1037/h0045925.

Bond, M. (2014). The secret of success. New Scientist, Vol. 221, Issue 2959, p. 30-34, 5p.

Brasseur, S., Gregoire, J., Bourdu, R., & Mikolajczak (2013). The profile of emotional competence (PEC): Development and validation of a self-reported measure that fits dimensions of emotional competence theory. PLOS, 8, 5, 1-8. Retrieved from www.plosone.org

Buscaglia, L. F. (1978). Personhood: The art of being fully human. New York: Ballantime Books.

Camileri, S., Caruanan, A., Falzon, R., & Muscat, M. (2012). The promotion of emotional literacy through personal and social development: The Maltese experience. Pastoral Care in Education, 30, 1, 19-37. doi:10.1080/02643944.2011.651223

Carson, B. (1992). Think big. Grand Rapids, Michigan: Zondervan Publishing House.

Chopra, D. (1994). The seven spiritual laws to success: A practical guide to the fulfillment of your dreams. San Rafael, CA: Amber-Allen Publishing.

Corey, G. (1996). Theory and practice of counseling and psychotherapy (5th ed.). Pacific Grove, CA.

Che, D. (2013). Total law of attraction: Unleash your secret creative power to get what you want. New York: Gallery Books.

Gold, L. (1959). Adler's theory of dreams: A holistic approach to interpretation. In B.B. Woman (Ed.), Handbook of dreams: Research, theories and applications (pp. 319-341). New York, NY: Van Nostrand Reinhold.

Hicks, E. & Hicks, J. (2006). The law of attraction: The basics of the teaching of Abraham. Carlsbad, CA: Hay House

Hill, P. L., Summer, R., & Burrow, A. L. (2014). Understanding the pathways to purpose: Examining personality and well-being correlates across adulthood. The Journal of Positive Psychology, 9, 3, 227-234. doi: 10.1080/17439760.2014.888587

Kass, J. (2001). Mentoring students in the development of leadership skills, health-promoting behavior, and pro-social behavior: A rationale for teaching contemplative practices in university education. Paper presented at the Colloquium on Contemplative Practice in Higher Education, Lesley University, Cambridge, Massachusetts.

Kimbro, D. (1997). What makes the great great? New York: Bantam Doubleday Deli Publishing Group.

Merriam – Webster online unabridged collegiate dictionary. Retrieved from http://unabridge.merriam-webster.com/cgi-bin/collegiate?va=success

Napoleon, H. (1937). Think and grow rich. New York: Penguin Group

New Testament. Tenn: The Gideons International.

Newman, B. M., & Newman, P. R. (1995). Development through life: A psychosocial approach (6th ed.). Pacific Groove, CA: Brooks/Cole.

Schaefer, S. M., Boylan, J. M., Van Reekum, C. M., Lapate, R. C., Norris, C. J., Ryff, C. D., & Davidson, R. J. (2013). Purpose in life predicts better emotional recovery from negative stimuli. PLOS ONE, 8, 11, 1-9. Retrieved from www.plosone.org

Schuller, R. (1985). The be-happy attitudes: Eight positive attitudes that can transform your life! USA: Library of Congress Cataloging in Publication Data.

Senge, P. M. (1990). The fifth discipline: The art of practice of learning organization. New York: Doubleday Currency

Singh, R. (1999). Live in a better way: Reflections on truth, love and happiness. New York: Penguin Putnam Inc.

Vanzant, I. (1993). Acts of Faith: Daily meditations for people of color. New York. Simon and Schuster.

Webster's New Dictionary (3rd ed.) New York: Simon and Schuster.

About the Author

Dr. Diane Davis was born and raised in Brooklyn, New York. Growing up with two other siblings, her parents ensured that education played a big role in their upbringing. In her early 20s she was faced with domestic violence, and struggled to find herself. She had gone to a revival tent, seeking God's help. At the tent, a pastor named Johnson had revealed that God had a higher calling for her to serve people. Through meditation, Dr. Davis heard a small voice telling her to follow this higher calling. She began helping others with only her high school diploma, and later attended graduate school. Dr. Davis attributes her success and perseverance to the hardships she herself has faced.

Driven by the desire to help others with their emotional and mental health, Dr. Davis is now a New York State Licensed Mental Health Counselor and member of the American Psychological Association. She maintains practice with Brooklyn Community Services, the Jewish Community Council of Greater New York, and Family Preservation Services of New York Corporation, for which she is the founder and clinician. Dr. Davis specializes in the treatment of depression, anxiety, grief, Post Traumatic Stress Disorder, and disruptive behavior disorders in children and adolescents. Dr. Davis received her Master's degree from Lincoln University and Doctoral degree from Capella University. Dr. Davis published her dissertation, "A Phenomenological Study of Middle School Adolescents: Understanding the Perspectives and Life Experiences that Contribute to Disruptive Behaviors". She is a Cognitive Behavioral trainer who leads groups in New York City with children and adolescents to help them change their negative thoughts, emotions, and disruptive behaviors into positive ones to live more full and abundant lives.

www.ingramcontent.com/pod-product-compliance
Lightning Source LLC
Chambersburg PA
CBHW070303010526
44108CB00039B/1709